THE TIME OF TROUBLES

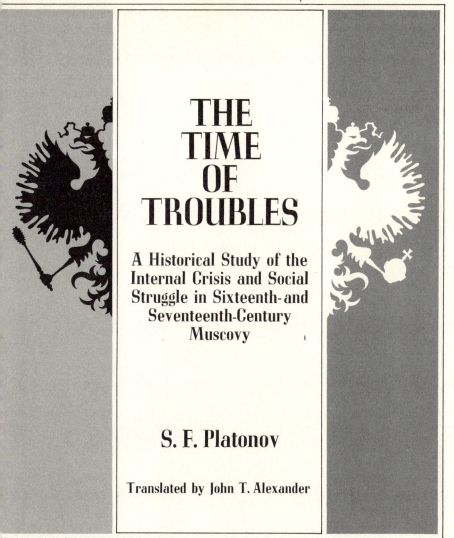

THE
TIME
OF
TROUBLES

A Historical Study of the Internal Crisis and Social Struggle in Sixteenth- and Seventeenth-Century Muscovy

S. F. Platonov

Translated by John T. Alexander

THE UNIVERSITY PRESS OF KANSAS │ LAWRENCE │ MANHATTAN │ WICHITA │ LONDON

to the memory of George C. Soulis | 1927•1966

Contents

Translator's Introduction

In the last thirty years or so the study of Russian history in the United States has undergone profound changes. Developing from modest but solid beginnings, it has now cast off an aura of the exotic in favor of the less glamorous but longer-lived attributes of an established field of study. No doubt the Cold War has stimulated such growth, particularly in the first postwar decade; and its impress shows up markedly in the high proportion of American scholars specializing in the study of twentieth-century Russia and the USSR. Indeed, if it were not for the virtual "schools" established by the late Professor Michael Karpovich at Harvard and Professor Emeritus George Vernadsky at Yale, the number of such scholars would probably be even larger.

Still, it seems evident that Russian history as a discipline in the United States needs more studies of the early modern, medieval, and ancient periods. The number of important works in English on the centuries of Russian history prior to 1800 remains miniscule. While numerous surveys and several sets of readings, useful to the student of earlier Russian history, are now easily available, there is a definite lack of medium-length studies of special periods. The present translation is intended to help remedy the shortage.

I decided to translate this particular work for several reasons. In broad terms it treats nearly a century and a half of Russian history (1500-1648);

in much greater detail it scrutinizes the crucial years of the national crisis in the Muscovite State popularly known as the Time of Troubles (1598-1613). Developments in this period highlight several major issues of Russian history: the growing consolidation of Muscovite absolutism and the formation of a national state; the expansion of Muscovy to the west and southeast; the demise of the boyar class and the rise of the service gentry; the emergence of serfdom as the social basis of Muscovite society; the cataclysmic end of one dynasty, the House of Rurik, and the beginnings of another, the House of Romanov. For Platonov—who devoted most of his career as a scholar to the study of these dramatic years—the epoch marked nothing less than the great divide between medieval Muscovy and modern Russia, witnessing the downfall of an essentially patrimonial regime and its replacement, after fierce struggles, by a more modern state founded on a new constellation of social groups.

Although the author's exposition is now almost fifty years old, most specialists outside the Soviet Union agree that Platonov's general treatment of the subject remains the most authoritative one. To be sure, during the last half-century, scholars have continued to work in this field. Recent research—mainly by Soviet scholars—has broadened our knowledge of the social, economic, and political history of medieval Muscovy; in particular, special studies by R. G. Skrynnikov, I. I. Smirnov, S. B. Veselovsky, and A. A. Zimin have thrown new light on Ivan the Terrible's oprichnina, Khlopko's "revolt," and the Bolotnikov rebellion. Nevertheless, beyond renaming the Time of Troubles "the period of the peasant war and foreign intervention," Soviet historiography has not fundamentally altered Platonov's interpretation. This is just as much a tribute to Platonov's remarkably sound and cautious scholarship as it is a reflection of the relative neglect of the period by subsequent scholarship.

Platonov's brief study also represents the finished product of a lifetime of research, writing, and teaching of Russian history. As such it constitutes a significant monument of modern Russian historiography. In his works Platonov synthesized, to a high degree, two major traditions of Russian historiography: the St. Petersburg "school," which emphasized the collection and rigorous use of primary sources, and the Moscow "school," with its socioeconomic and geopolitical approaches. Several of his interpretations, particularly his treatment of the oprichnina and of Boris Godunov, represented important revisions of previous historiography and have since become widely accepted. Finally, Platonov's book offers a masterfully concise and cogent exposition of its subject, a quality that time has not tarnished.

Born in 1860, the son of a city workman whose father was a serf, Sergei Feodorovich Platonov attained in his lifetime immense public and professional recognition in his country as a leading authority on Russian history. Both his published university lectures and his textbook for secondary schools went through more than ten editions. Even his Master's dissertation, a specialized investigation of seventeenth-century Muscovite sources, became such a bibliographical treasure that it required a second printing. Altogether his books, articles, and published lectures totaled more than one hundred separate titles. Like many Russian intellectuals, moreover, Platonov was exceptionally active in a variety of spheres. For nearly thirty years he held the chair of Russian history at St. Petersburg University, where he helped to train an entire generation of Russian historians. At the same time he edited several large collections of sources, and for ten years he was closely associated with the editorial board of the *Zhurnal Ministerstva Narodnago Prosveshcheniia* [Journal of the Ministry of Public Education], an outstanding scholarly publication of the era. During his long career he also lectured at many secondary schools in the Imperial capital, tutored several children of the Romanov family, and for thirteen years directed a women's pedagogical institute. In 1920 he participated as an expert in the negotiations for the Treaty of Riga between the Soviet Union and Poland. Retired from teaching in 1916, Platonov became a full member of the Academy of Sciences in 1920 and served until 1929 as director of its library and head of its research institute, Pushkin House.

Today, however, Platonov is an almost forgotten figure in the Soviet Union. He died in 1933 while in forced exile at faraway Samara (now Kuibyshev) on the Volga—one of many tragic victims of the general regimentation imposed on Soviet cultural life at the end of the 1920's. Ironically, so far the only one of his works republished under the Soviet regime was issued in 1937, at the height of the Great Purges. Outside Russia, Platonov's writings have not enjoyed the wide appreciation given those of his renowned compatriot V. O. Kliuchevsky. Indeed, the masterpiece upon which his claim to greatness principally rests, his superb *Outlines of the History of the Troubles in the Muscovite State in the Sixteenth and Seventeenth Centuries* (St. Petersburg, 1899; plus two subsequent editions and a fourth printing), has never been translated. To my knowledge, only five of Platonov's other publications have been translated into Western languages (just one into English), but none of these is recent or widely available in the United States. He deserves better of posterity.

The work translated here is Platonov's short study, *Smutnoe vremia* [The Time of Troubles] (Petersburg, 1923; Prague, 1924), which represents a condensation and popularization of his larger work mentioned above. The Prague edition has been used, and all quotations and ellipses are present in the original (since the book is addressed to a broad audience, Platonov did not include citations of sources). In translating Platonov's prose I have attempted to remain true to his meaning, but I have taken some liberties with phrasing, sentence structure, and paragraphing in order to render his text more intelligible to the nonspecialist reader who knows no Russian. I have accepted the customary translation of *Smuta* and *Smutnoe vremia* as Troubles and Time of Troubles, respectively, though I have also rendered the former as confusion, turbulence, turmoil, etc. In addition, I have supplied a few explanatory items in brackets and in footnotes, the latter being distinguished from the author's own by the use of arabic numerals and the symbol (T.). Since this translation is directed to the nonspecialist, I have translated several Russian technical terms and titles; however, some well-known and frequently repeated terms—such as boyar, mir, oprichnina, posad, voevoda, Zemsky Sobor, etc.—have simply been anglicized. In a few cases, as a means of indicating the technical nature of certain terms, I have enclosed them in quotation marks, e.g., "black lands," although these are absent in the Russian text. A short glossary of these terms has been appended. In other cases, when Platonov quoted a term from contemporary sources for which I could not devise a translation of comparable color and force, I have simply translated the word and omitted the quotation marks. And since I am not myself a specialist on the period this book covers, I have made no attempt to update or to correct Platonov in the light of subsequent scholarship.

I have generally followed the Library of Congress system of transliteration, with a few common variations: the omission of ligatures and of hard and soft signs; the use of -y instead of -ii at the end of words, and an initial ya and yu instead of ia and iu. The soft sign preceding the vowel e has been rendered as i, hence Pomorie rather than Pomor'e; other soft signs have been omitted. Furthermore, the spelling of several names has been entirely exempted from the system, since it has been sanctioned by time and popular usage. Thus Dimitry, Moscow, Peter, Cossack, Ivan the Terrible, Sigismund, Hermogen, and Feodor have retained their customary forms. Unlike the author, who used Russian spelling throughout, I have rendered Polish names as they are spelled in Polish—thus Wladyslaw, not Vladislav; Sapieha, not Sapega or Sopega, etc. (I recognize that in the case of persons from Lithuania this may imply rather arbitrary judgments as to nationality, even though such are not intended.) A selection of readings in English has been included to aid readers who wish to investigate the subject further.

Many persons have assisted in the preparation of this translation. I am deeply grateful to Professor Oswald P. Backus, III, my distinguished senior colleague at the University of Kansas, and to Mr. Sergei Pushkarev, of New Haven, Connecticut. Both of these scholars carefully read my text, checked it against the original, and saved me from numerous errors. Two other colleagues—Professor Theodore A. Wilson, of the University of Kansas, and Professor Herbert J. Ellison, of the University of Washington—generously helped to improve the English style of the text. At an earlier stage my father, Dr. Edward P. Alexander, read most of the text and offered numerous suggestions. The late Professor George C. Soulis encouraged me to undertake this project and also read an early draft of chapter three, while Dr. Fritz T. Epstein, of Indiana University, offered much friendly guidance and moral support. Professor Edward Keenan, of Harvard University, aided in the translation of quotations from Old Russian, as did Professors Walter N. Vickery and John F. Beebe, both then at Indiana University. Professors Robert F. Byrnes and John M. Thompson, my mentors in Russian history at Indiana University, have displayed a serious interest in this project throughout its preparation. I am also indebted to numerous secretaries who have typed and retyped the manuscript, often on very short notice, and to the Foreign Area Fellowship Program whose generous fellowship aid made it possible for me to complete this work. Like all authors, I am particularly appreciative of the expert help I have received from the personnel of the University Press of Kansas, especially its director, Mr. John Dessauer, its senior editor, Mrs. Yvonne Willingham, and its designer, Professor Frank Reiber. Finally, for her inspiration, numerous suggestions, and—above all— great patience, my wife, Maria K. Alexander, de- serves immeasurable gratitude. Whatever errors and imperfections remain are, of course, my own responsibility.

John T. Alexander
Lawrence, Kansas

Author's Preface

The aim of the present book is to give a brief and connected account of the events of the Time of Troubles, which the Muscovite State passed through at the turn of the sixteenth and seventeenth centuries. The author has tried to construct his account so as to acquaint the reader not only with the course of the Muscovite Troubles, but also with their origin and results. Remaining strictly factual, this exposition is not subordinated to any preconceived point of view, either subjectivist or theoretical. The author wished to remain only a chronicler of the epoch, leaving the reader free to interpret the facts presented.

In comparison to the author's larger work on the same subject, the present brief study differs somewhat both in plan and execution. The former was written a quarter of a century ago, and many of its details have been revised by later researchers; moreover, in connection with the tricentennial of the Troubles, new materials relating to their history have been found and published. Therefore, several changes have become necessary in the elucidation of details of the epoch. Furthermore, the author considered it superfluous to repeat the cumbersome geographical survey of the Muscovite State which prefaced the larger study, and so he has replaced it with an introduction of a type suitable for a popular work.

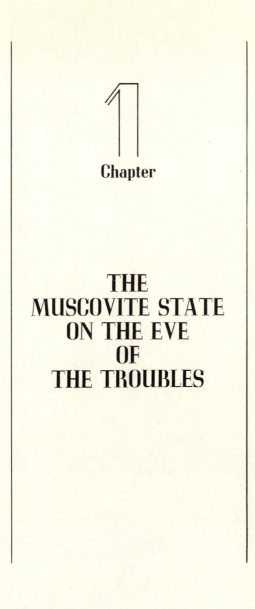

Chapter

THE
MUSCOVITE STATE
ON THE EVE
OF
THE TROUBLES

I

The Muscovite State formed from two "halves":

1. The Lower Land or Zamoskovie: the colonization of the region and princely appanages; the formation of a national state.

2. Novgorod Land: the character of Novgorod's commerce; the Novgorod aristocracy and the colonization of the North; the conquest by Muscovy.

1

At the end of the fifteenth and the beginning of the sixteenth century Muscovites pictured their state as a compound structure. In their minds it was divided into two "halves" —Novgorod Land and the Lower[1] or Muscovite Land. Such a conception was based not only upon Moscow's success in conquering the entire Novgorod State, but also upon certain peculiarities of internal structure preserved in these "halves" after their unification under one power, peculiarities not immediately effaced by the harsh hand of the Muscovite government. Moscow dealt sternly with Novgorod's institutions, and they disappeared very rapidly. But their basis—the natural geographical conditions of economic life—remained the old one, and it continued to influence the course of local life and social relationships. The whole history of the settlement and economic development of the Novgorod and Muscovite "halves" had followed different paths. Novgorod had rapidly completed a fast-paced cycle of internal development, and its social and political order had begun to decay even before the external

---

1. "Lower" presumably in a geographical sense, i.e., lying to the south of Novgorod. (T.).

enemy shattered it. In contrast, the Lower or Muscovite half of Great Russia had been formed more slowly, and under the influence of external danger it had organized a single powerful principality which preserved early forms of social intercourse. United into one state, the "halves" did not assimilate immediately. Regional peculiarities were very noticeable in them; their social structures were different, and for this reason the Troubles of the first years of the seventeenth century occurred in each quite differently. We must acquaint ourselves with the distinctive modes of local life in the Muscovite and Novgorod regions in order to understand clearly the complex process of the Troubles which erupted in them.

We shall begin with the Lower Land, which later received the name "Zamoskovie."[2] Under these designations were subsumed the lands of the old "great princedoms": Vladimir, Moscow, Rostov, Suzdal, Nizhny Novgorod, and Tver, which together constituted the Great Russian heartland. They had long since possessed a dense population and a comparatively well-developed economy, with much industrial and commercial activity. This whole expanse had begun to be settled by Russian tribes only in historic times, at first by settlers from the northern, and then also from the southern, Russian principalities. The oldest towns founded here had shown evidence of rapid growth and energetic culture in the pre-Tatar era. They immediately provided the local princes with substantial means and raised their political significance to a great height, so that at the close of the twelfth and the beginning of the thirteenth century the princes of Vladimir were the most powerful in all Russia. In literary monuments of that time rapturous wonderment at the political and cultural activities of these princes is frequently revealed. The prince of Vladimir, according to the lay of an ancient poet, was so mighty that he could "with his oars scatter in drops the Volga, and with his helmets scoop dry the Don." The artistic taste and

---

2. That is, "land beyond the Moskva River," to the north and east of Moscow. (T.)

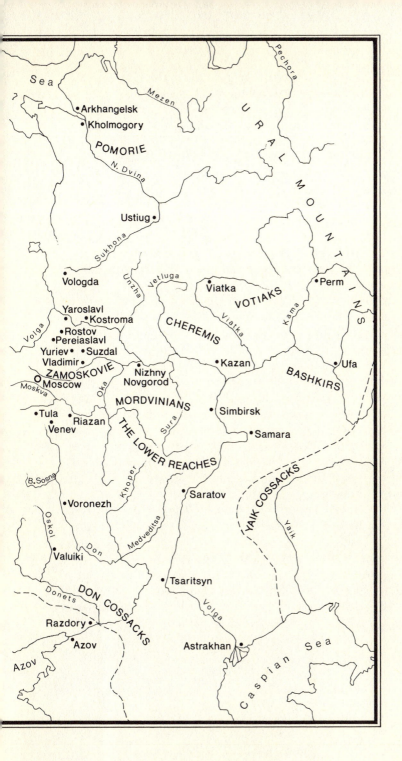

material wealth of the northern princes captivated the chroniclers; with rapture they mention the princely churches of Rostov and Vladimir, saying that "master craftsmen from all lands" had labored over them, and that the churches were so "wondrous and great" that there had never been such before nor would be again. All this power and magnificence was suddenly destroyed in the middle of the thirteenth century by the devastating Tatar [Mongol] invasion. Tatar power cut off the Russia of Vladimir-Suzdal from its ties with the contemporary cultural centers of the south and west and turned eastern Great Russia into a backwoods borderland. The country's political life stagnated, commerce languished. The general devastation brought with it the decline of the towns and the dispersal of their population. In short, the whole land gradually turned into a group of dissociated appanages, in which sat proprietor-princes who warred with each other and only worried about their own "acquisitions," that is, their own profit and the strengthening of their own territories at the expense of the others. Almost brought to a halt by the Tatar invasion, the colonizing movement from the western and southwestern Russian regions revived and, turning toward the north and northeast, gradually extended the area of Russian settlement beyond the Volga and into the lower reaches of the Oka. The appanage princes not only took an active part in this movement; they built their entire economy and administration, so to speak, upon it, for they lived in complete dependence on the advancing frontier.

Someone has aptly likened the appanage prince of northern Russia to a willow growing on the banks of a flowing stream. Just as an immobile tree feeds its roots and moistens its foliage from the very waters that its branches shade, so too the prince, living a settled life on his appanage "patrimony," had to nourish himself from the human stream, not being strong enough to stop or to direct it. The human stream flowed into this land across its western and southern borders and proceeded toward the White Sea and the "Rockies" (Urals). It was neither the headlong movement of migrating masses nor the passage of wandering nomads; rather it was a slow, elemental migration of tilling folk from clearing to clearing behind leaders of various types. Sometimes this leader was the prince himself who acquired new "patrimonies" in the wild places of the non-Russian North. Sometimes monks or hermits indicated the paths of migration, going off from settled areas "for silence" to the wooded wilderness and against their will attracting after them plowmen to new, worthwhile "starts." And sometimes the peasant entrepreneur and the hunter searching for prey set their traps and traplines in the forest and founded a new settlement, to which the neighboring peasantry then began to be drawn. Silently and imperceptibly the laboring population diffused through the country, seeking application of its labor in the dense thickets of the forests, on the loamy and sandy soils of the river valleys, and along the shores of the lakes and the rivers. There were no special impediments to the movement; it freely advanced along the northern rivers even to the shores of the White Sea, searching for furs and falcons for princely and boyar hunting. But only isolated parties got that far; the bulk of them bogged down in the Trans-Volga region, in the forest wilds of the watershed between the Volga and the rivers of the *Pomorie*, [3] and were long held there by the resistance of the native peoples along the Vetluga-Sura line. Between the rivers Unzha and Vetluga "the Cheremis war raged unceasingly," and the Unzha forests remained impassable for the Russian plowman and hunter. And further to the south, between the Oka and the Sura, the Mordvinians prevented Russian settlement. Nizhny Novgorod long stood as the demarcation point separating the Russia of the Volga from the non-Russian Lower Reaches.

The princes of this Russia of the Volga had to build their economy and governmental order under conditions of

---

3. *Pomorie*, literally "region along the sea," referred to the northern region of European Russia bordering on the White Sea and the Arctic Ocean and extending several hundred miles inland. (T.)

uninterrupted population movement. Since the princes were not strong enough to restrain or to bind the mass of the people to one place, they adapted to the latter's "fluid state" (as S. M. Soloviev has expressed it). In a principality only the princely court was settled and fixed. It included servants of the prince—free (boyars and *deti boyarskie*[4]) and unfree ("people" or slaves). Both the former and the latter lived in personal dependence upon the prince, bound to him either by a contract of service or by the chains of slavery. They constituted the council of the prince, his administration, his army, his labor force. They were all registered and could only leave the princely court with the agreement or knowledge of their lord.

It was quite different outside the prince's court. Besides the lands in the princely appanage which belonged directly to the prince, there were, first, church or boyar lands, the administration of which followed the pattern of the princely court, and second, "black lands," on which peasants lived—"on the sovereign's land, but in their own settlement." The inhabitants of the first kind of lands, church or boyar peasants, were shielded from the prince by their lords and owners, and princely agents could not "come to them for anything." On the lands of the second order, however, under the supervision of the prince's agents (stewards, prefects, and so on) had developed peasant self-government, the organs of which shielded each member of the peasant commune from the influence of the princely power. A peasant *"mir"* [commune] most frequently grouped itself around a church built by the *"mir,"* corresponding in its composition to a church parish. Several neighboring *"mirs,"* joined in a unit for purposes of taxation, constituted a rural district [*volost'*], which sometimes attained great complexity of composition and encompassed a large expanse of "black lands." The population of such districts changed in its quantity and personal composition independently of the prince and without his knowledge. The coloni-

---

4. Literally "boyar sons," this was a lower rank of Muscovite service gentry. (T.)

zation process brought settlers to a district and took them away spontaneously. The new settler, arriving at the borders of a district, was enrolled and assigned a plot of land by the elected communal authorities—the "elders of the land"—and pledged or obligated himself to them "to bear the burden of all tax collections equally with the other members of the *mir*." Accepted into the *"mir,"* the peasant made himself at home in his new settlement and in the course of time became an "old-dweller" [5] of that district.

If, however, the peasant could not sustain himself on the new land, he "renounced" before the same elders and, having fulfilled all the customary formalities for "departure," left the district in search of a new piece of land. His arrival in the district, like his exit from it, did not concern the prince. In his migration from place to place the peasant wandered from one princely appanage to another, unaware that he was crossing political borders and thus changing his allegiance. The very concept of allegiance, in the sense of a compulsory subordination to authority, did not exist in those times, and "sovereign" [*gosudar'*] then did not denote the head of a principality, but the head of a separate patrimonial economy in relation to the people under his civil authority. The slave had a sovereign-owner over him; the free man, however, in addressing a prince named him simply "Lord Prince" [*gospodin kniaz'*], and in changing the prince over him by altering his place of labor he had no thought of committing "treason." The prince, by the same token, did not know when such a free peasant arrived on his appanage or when he left. If the *"mir"* set up impediments to the peasant's "departure," these sprang from economic rather than political causes—in cases when the emigrant tried to leave at other than the customary time (St. George's Day, November 26), without settling accounts with the *"mir,"* or

---

5. In contrast to newcomers, who were often attracted to new lands by advances, promises of tax remission, and so forth, "old-dwellers" [*starozhil'tsy*] were liable for the full amount of taxes and dues to their lords and to the state. (T.)

without observing the customary forms of "renunciation." A peasant who did not leave his plot properly was denominated a fugitive and by custom was liable to be returned to his "old hearth" for the fulfillment of the obligations he had assumed. In other cases he was not compelled to return.

Under such conditions the prince did not have the slightest possibility of making an exact count of the population of the peasant "black-land" districts or of binding these people to their place of labor. Rather than counting people, he limited himself to enumerating homesteads or households, plowed land, and other appurtenances, [6] and in proportion to these imposed a single tax payment upon an entire district. It was left to the local population itself to apportion this assessment among the individual units. In exactly the same general manner the prince also determined all the duties and services which he demanded from a district to supplement the money payment. Thus was determined the composition of the total "burden" [*tiaglo*] which fell upon a rural district. How it was divided among individual taxpayers the prince need not know. So long as the "burden" was furnished punctually he was not interested in whether the number of taxpayers in a given district increased or decreased, and did not try to restrain emigrants unless the district itself requested him to do so.

Such was the simplest kind of appanage principality— that political form out of which the Muscovite State gradually emerged. In the first stages of its formation this state had itself been a large appanage and only quantitatively distinguished from other, smaller and poorer, appanages. In the course of time a qualitative difference also appeared. From the beginning of the fifteenth century a perceptible sense of national consciousness arose in the country, and Moscow became the center of a nationality in search of unity. The grand prince of

---

6. The Russian term *ugodia* is equivalent to the old English legal term "uses"; it encompassed privileges to all kinds of productive and profitable resources, e.g., hunting places, fisheries, beehives, etc. (T.)

Moscow acted as a leader of the people of his generation in the struggle with their traditional foes, chiefly the Tatars.

New tasks also demanded new means for their solution. The patriarchal forms of an appanage economy were unsuited for the realization of national political aims. So the Muscovite authorities began to strive for a new order. It became their ideal to bind the elements of society to their obligations—rendering service and paying taxes. Instead of free agents living with the prince by contract, boyars and free servitors were obliged to become his "slaves," subjects powerless to leave the sovereign's service and subordinate to his will. "Burdened" people were obliged to stay firmly on their land, to live where the state census-taker found them and registered them in the cadastral book. Those unattached elements of the "burdened *mirs*" still able to wander as "people unburdened and unregistered"—namely, "sons living with fathers, nephews living with uncles, and unenrolled peasants living with neighbors"—gradually had to settle on their own or another's land and no longer "wander between households." Of course, this ideal was not easily realized: it is impossible by command alone to arrest spontaneity and to force a human mass immediately to congeal into desired forms. The boyars and servitors tried to fight for the old rights and liberties, while as before the peasantry "abandoned their huts and wandered off." But the central power rapidly, in the course of three or four generations in all, achieved great results. Around the grand prince of Moscow there appeared a broad and compact circle of boyars, the majority of whom were devoted to Moscow and proud that its representatives had "from time immemorial served none other than their lords," the princes of Moscow. Below this service class of aristocracy in the capital was formed a provincial category of servitors—the *deti boyarskie* and the gentry [*dvoriane*]. In rare cases they lived on their own patrimonies (that is, hereditary lands). Yet the great bulk of them, amounting to many thousands, were granted tenurial privileges on the sovereign's land (called *pomestie* land) and held it in return for service. Vast expanses of "black land" (and likewise crown land) passed out of the hands of the peasantry into those of the service gentry, the *"pomeshchiks* of the grand prince." All the border regions of the state and its entire center were covered with small pomestie estates, and in place of peasant self-government the initial form of serfdom was established.

Settling pomeshchiks in a rural district and distributing small portions of peasant communal lands to them, the grand prince indicated the limits of the pomeshchik's authority thus: "And it is for you, peasants, to serve him, your lord, and to do field work for him, the lord, and to pay him everything that he, the lord, shall demand of you in place of labor." Himself bound to the estate, the pomeshchik in turn bound the peasant to it. Furnishing his grand prince military power, the pomeshchik also provided him with the necessary administrative power that could fix the taxpayers in their places. By these and other similar methods, the Muscovite central authorities gradually crystallized the population, transforming it from the fluid state of the appanage epoch. The grand prince even tried to account for dependent people on private estates, demanding that those who entered into slavery be registered with government agents. Directly or indirectly the entire population of the state became subject to the Muscovite sovereign. In this lay the principal import of the Muscovite measures.

At the close of the fifteenth century Muscovite Russia formed a large state, with a powerful supreme power and a clearly expressed national idea. Having united around himself the entire Great Russian nationality, the grand prince of Moscow, according to V. O. Kliuchevsky, "was moving toward democratic sovereignty." Having annexed to his own hereditary appanage all the other Great Russian appanages, he considered himself the owner, in personal tenure, of the land he held. "Our patrimony," he declared, "is not just the towns and districts presently held by us, but all the Russian land from antiquity, from our forefathers, is our patrimony." The proprietary character of Muscovite authority lent it patriarchal features; it preserved in the Muscovite state order a certain measure of private economic relationships. In short, the appanage past still lived on in Muscovite institutions and class relationships. But the national upsurge which had forged Great Russian unity won for the sovereign of Muscovy the lofty role of a popular leader, who was supported by the whole mass of the people and who was leading them not only to national unity but also to international primacy among all "Orthodoxy," that is, to a leading role among all the other nationalities of the Greek Orthodox Church.

A completely different picture was presented during the same epoch by "Lord Novgorod the Great."

2

The history of the formation of the Novgorod State is generally known. By gradually strengthening and broadening their self-government at the expense of their prince's personal rule, the Novgorodians succeeded in creating a special political order. Princely rule by inheritance was ended, and the Novgorodians summoned princes from outside according to their choice. Supreme power belonged to the *veche,* which by its own conception consisted not of individuals but of those organizations—wards, streets, and so on—that made up the city-state of Great Novgorod. The leader of the veche was the governing council—"the lords"—in which sat the prince, the archbishop, the incumbent *posadnik,* and all the old posadniks (elected leaders of civil administration in Novgorod). In theory, any freeman who possessed even the slightest property qualification (a household) could participate in the government of his country. In fact, however, power was held by Novgorod's aristocracy—the boyars and the well-to-do people. This was an aristocracy of capital. When it degenerated into an oligarchy of a small circle of the richest families, the country lapsed into chronic internecine strife between the ruling boyars and the deprived mass of the people. This process of transition from

democracy to oligarchy and the disintegration of the governmental order was completed very rapidly (as early as the fourteenth century), and had its roots in the peculiarities of Novgorod's economic life.

All the country subordinate to Novgorod, known as
"fifths," [7] extended from the Onegan inlets of the White Sea
through the district of lakes Ladoga, Onega, and Ilmen to the
watershed of the Ilmen rivers and the Western Dvina. Its central line, from north to south, was formed by the Volkhov and
Lovat rivers. To the west of that line were many towns—fortified places. They protected Novgorod from its external foes
and constituted a good system of defense. But all of them, with
the exception of Pskov and Staraia Russa, were economically
insignificant. To the east of the Volkhov-Lovat line there were
no towns at all, and the little settlements that substituted for
them were insignificant both in terms of population and their
importance for the life of the region. The territory of
Novgorod was sparsely settled, and all its population—especially the most active classes—was concentrated in only three
points: Novgorod proper, Pskov, and Staraia Russa. The latter
possessed more than 1,500 households and equalled in population the largest towns of Muscovite Russia—Yaroslavl, Vologda, and Nizhny Novgorod. In number of households both
Novgorod and Pskov apparently surpassed even Moscow and
were the largest towns in all of ancient Russia; in fifteenth-
century Novgorod there were as many as 6,000 households, in
Pskov nearly 7,000. According to European standards of that
epoch these were some of the most significant towns in Europe.
Thus the Novgorod State (Pskov became independent in the
fourteenth century) developed a peculiar irregularity in the
distribution of its population: the capital swallowed up, as it
were, all the resources of the land, leaving very little to the
provinces. It concentrated in itself all trade and all industries,
and became in this regard like an oasis in a desert.

---

7. Because it was divided into five large territorial subdivisions. (T.)

The causes of such concentration of economic power lay in the basic characteristics of Novgorod's state territory. With the exception of small stretches to the extreme south, the entire Novgorod country was barren. It gave lean harvests, and frequently none at all if frost killed the spring barley. Against their will Novgorodians had to cultivate the earth, for they could not rely upon the regular import of grain from the Russian south and east. In better conditions the people of Novgorod would have undertaken entirely different forms of labor; but as long as the eastern and southern princes had the possibility of "cutting the path" to Novgorod and obstructing import into the city, the Novgorodians had to man the plow and "suffer" on the meager soil. Nevertheless, agriculture was only a secondary support to them; primary importance in Novgorod's economic life belonged to trade and to those industries that fed it. These industries furnished valuable goods to the Novgorod market: furs, wax, salt, sea animals, train oil, and fish. To obtain them within the bounds of the "fifths" was impossible; one had to go to sea and into the northern forests, where valuable game was still to be found in fabulous abundance. A Novgorod folk tale tells of the incredible wealth of the North, where as if from the clouds small squirrels and reindeer fell to earth and dispersed about the land. In search of this wealth Novgorodians early journeyed to the distant North, severe but abundant, and seized for themselves huge expanses along the shores of the White Sea. The new lands provided valuable goods for the Novgorod market. From Novgorod the products were shipped "beyond the sea" to Europe, to the "Germans."[8] In exchange Hanseatic and Swedish merchants brought cloth, wine, spices, and metals to Novgorod. The Novgorodians distributed the wares "from beyond the sea" to the Russian south and east, receiving mainly grain in return. Thus, in the circulation of its commerce

---

8. Muscovites termed northern and western Europeans "Germans," *nemtsy* (from *nemoi*—mute), since they usually did not speak or understand Russian. (T.)

Novgorod supplied nothing from its own soil. It served only as an intermediary between its northern colonies, Central Europe, and Russia, and drew its profit from the very nature of its middleman role. Novgorod was an extremely important marketing point, where the Pomorie, Russian, and "German" goods met, and where large-scale transactions took place. And it was this international market which attracted all the active elements of Novgorod's population, leaving in the "fifths" only "lesser" people—agriculturalists and fishermen. Pskov alone shared commercial leadership of the country with Novgorod and rivaled it as an entrepôt for trade beyond the sea. The remainder of the country submissively looked to Novgorod and was drawn by all interests to its market.

The character and organization of Novgorod's commerce determined the importance of its aristocracy—the boyars and the well-to-do people. Commercial hegemony belonged to them, and all stages of Novgorod's trade cycle were under their direction. The procurement of goods in the far North and their delivery to Novgorod required large means and solid organization. Transactions with foreign buyers well organized in their own right required that the mutual relations between Novgorodian and "German" merchants be carefully defined. Under the conditions of the time the small manufacturer and trader could not alone muster strength enough to produce, deliver, and sell small lots of goods. Armed force was often necessary to maintain a place of production and means of communication in the non-Russian North; tremendous efforts were necessary to transport goods over marshy portages and rivers filled with rapids; and at the Novgorod market itself the Russian merchant met wily and shrewd "Germans"—contractors, buyers, and sellers who closely watched over their own interests and who were tightly united by a corporative bond. In this situation only economically powerful and politically influential people could operate with success—people such as the boyars and the well-to-do groups of Novgorod. In the North they seized tremendous expanses of land for their holdings, settled them with their slaves, and at their production sites exploited the local native population—the Lapps and the Karelians. They ruled the market in Novgorod itself, filled it with their goods, and made the commercial middlemen, the merchants, dependent upon them. In their own interests they created this or that political situation, influencing the "arrangements" (treaties) with Russian princes and foreigners. Finally, they shackled the population of the "fifths" economically as well, acquiring land there and renting it out to small tenants who were completely dependent upon their great lords. In the course of only two centuries the economic hegemony of the Novgorod aristocracy reached the stage of a political dictatorship. In the fifteenth century Novgorod began to be governed by a small clique of boyar families in whose hands were concentrated all the means of influencing the masses. In their internecine strife they incited the mob against their foes and plunged the city into anarchy. Perpetual disturbances began in Novgorod, and the deprived mass of the populace, hating the boyars, was ready at any moment to rise up against them.

This state of affairs in Novgorod was exploited by Moscow. It intervened in Novgorod's affairs at the behest of the lower strata of the local population, and its initial activities in subjugated Novgorod were directed against the boyars. The grand prince of Moscow gradually, though rapidly enough, annihilated Novgorod's boyar class. The means for this were direct denouncements, sometimes crowned by executions, but more frequently used was the celebrated "deportation" which Moscow liked to employ in relations with subjugated regions. Grand Prince Ivan III at first promised the boyars of Novgorod not to remove them: "We grant this favor to our patrimony" [i.e., Novgorod], he said in 1478, "that they should not fear deportation and we shall not trespass upon their patrimonies." But later, when boyar plots were discovered in Novgorod in 1484 and 1489, the grand prince changed his mind: "He transferred from Great Novgorod many boyars and well-to-do people and great merchants, in all more than a thousand," recounts the chronicler of the year 1489, "and granted them pomestie estates in Moscow, and in Vladimir, and in Murom, and in Nizhny Novgorod, and in Pereiaslavl, and in Yuriev, and in Rostov, and in Kostroma, and in other towns; while to their estates in Novgorod the Great he sent many of the best people of Muscovy, merchants and *deti boyarskie,* and from other towns in his Muscovite patrimonies [he sent] many *deti boyarskie* and merchants." This was the very same measure that Moscow had used so successfully and rapidly to assimilate its conquests. Within a quarter century of Novgorod's annexation to Moscow, "the boyarlings of Novgorod had all been got rid of," and boyar landholding had disappeared, to be replaced by the small pomestie estates of Muscovite servitors. Meanwhile the *smerds* (peasants) of Novgorod, who had been living on land leased from the boyars, were, in the end, following the Muscovite pattern, bound to the pomestie estates of the *deti boyarskie* of the grand sovereign. Thus the physiognomy of Novgorod's "fifths" changed. And with it changed the Novgorodian North.

Under the Novgorodian regime the North had been a non-Russian, sparsely settled region, which the Russian population of Novgorod had colonized. The principal motive of settlement had been the search for goods to supply the Novgorod market; the leaders of the movement had been the boyars of Novgorod, who controlled that market; the predominant form of Russian colonization in the North had been the production site, a camp of hunters or fishermen; and in the first period most of the settlers had been boyars' people—slaves working for their lords. Primacy in the mastery of the Pomorie had belonged to them. They were soon followed by different settlers: the free plowman and the hermit-monk, who worked on small plots for themselves, or in small companies of a few or several friends. Out of these elements there slowly developed, over the centuries, that free population of the Pomorie which formed the democratic base of Russian population in the region—the peasants in their parishes and rural districts, the monks in their monasteries. When with the fall of Novgorodian authority the region came into Muscovite hands, Moscow did not send its pomeshchiks there, for the absence of foes in the North made this unnecessary. The peasant *"mirs"* were left with their already existing communal self-government. And the population of boyar territories, freed from boyar rule, was brought under the same forms of the peasant rural district. The entire North henceforth became a region of free peasantry. Only a few wealthy monasteries represented large-scale landholding there, but usually they, too, retained on their lands the communal peasant organization under the supervision of monastic authorities.

II

In the sixteenth century all the basic regions of the Muscovite State experience a crisis.
1. The princely aristocracy and the oprichnina of Ivan the Terrible.
2. The pomestie system and peasant bondage.
3. Peasant "departure" and the desolation of the Muscovite center.
4. The Muscovite town in the sixteenth century.

1

And so, by the beginning of the sixteenth century there had evolved within the Muscovite State, in both of its "halves," three regions that were virtually distinct from one another in their internal features: the heartland of the state (or Zamoskovie), the Novgorod "fifths," and the North—the Pomorie (by which we mean all the area along the seashores and in the valleys of the northern rivers). In the sixteenth century important changes occurred in the life of these regions causing a grave social crisis in Zamoskovie and the Novgorod "fifths." At the same time, in the middle of the sixteenth century the successful policy of Moscow added to the three basic regions of the state two more: the middle and lower Volga region and the southern "Field."[9] Both in the Volga region and, in particular, on the Field a somewhat special social structure was created, dependent to a significant degree upon the changes taking place in the central regions. The observer who wishes to reduce to some general characterization the internal processes of Muscovite life in the sixteenth century is unwittingly astonished by their complexity and diversity. As early as the middle of the century he can detect symptoms of the threatening social collapse that propelled the state into the Troubles.

Of these processes the most noticeable was what we may call the persecution of the princely aristocracy. With the annexation to Moscow of the appanage lands, their rulers, the appanage princes, became dependent upon the sovereigns of Moscow "and enrolled in their service." At first the service princes were kept separate from the Muscovite boyars, and the group surrounding the sovereign in Moscow was officially termed "the princes and the boyars." In the course of time the Muscovite service order assimilated the appanage princes and their posterity; they began to receive councillors' and court ranks on par with the boyars and were mixed with the untitled boyars into a single group of servitors. The custom of *mestnichestvo* ("order of precedence," or rank according to degree of aristocracy) arranged this group into definite layers. On top were the most eminent princes of the blood ("the elder brethren"); below them were the most noble and ancient families of Muscovite boyars—"the sovereign's from time immemorial,"

9. The "Wild Field" denoted the unsettled steppe region extending south from about present-day Tula. (T.)

who had "never served another" except the sovereigns of Moscow. Next came titled and simple service families with less eminence (or genealogical status) on down to the "poor little princelings" who had lost their property and social standing amidst the unfavorable conditions of Muscovite life and service. Upon entering the corps of Muscovite boyars, however, the princely aristocracy did not forget its dynastic origins or its proprietary habits. Several "princes of the blood" [*kniazhata*] remembered that they were descended from even older princely lines than the Muscovite sovereigns. Remnants of the appanage order preserved for these princes in their hereditary lands the proprietary rights which had made them "sovereigns" in their princely patrimonies. They had their own "court," their own servitors; they themselves judged the population of their lands; they "granted" villages and meadows out of their lands to churches and to individuals. According to the formula of one contemporary, they were "sovereigns of all the Russian lands," dependent only on the grand prince of Moscow, who was "the sovereign over the sovereigns of all the Russian lands."

Princely "pedigree" and princely patrimonies formed the foundations of the princely group and made their position in Muscovy independent of the sovereign's personal discretion. "For service the sovereign grants pomestie estates and monies, but not family [status]," it was said then, and therefore men of high pedigree imperiously expected "because of their family" the leading positions, quarreled over them, and to gain them sought neither the will nor the favor of the grand sovereign. The sovereigns could exile and even execute individual princes who displeased them, but they could not eliminate the entire group of princely aristocracy from governmental primacy, nor could they possibly rule the state without this class. In order to liberate the monarch from the collaboration of this unreliable and discomfiting handmaiden, some kind of general measure was necessary. The Muscovite grand princes did not hit upon this, however, until the middle of the sixteenth century.

They grappled more decisively with princely patrimonies. From the time of Ivan III [1462-1505] limiting statutes about such patrimonies have been preserved. The princes were forbidden to dispose of their lands freely, to sell or to will them; the government occasionally resorted to confiscation of princely lands, or sometimes exchanged them for other estates from its fund of land. The jealous and suspicious attention of the central authorities to princely landholding is readily understandable. The great patrimonial estates of the princes formed the basis of their economic power, and the government was apprehensive lest in time of need the princes employ the population subject to them to wage a political struggle against Moscow. At times the oppositionist tendencies of the princes became manifest; their traditional aspiration to share rulership with the sovereign remained constant. During Ivan the Terrible's youth this tendency on the part of the princes shown forth especially clearly in the activities of the so-called "Chosen Council"—that intimate circle of courtiers that was formed under the direction of "Priest Sylvester" to assist the impressionable and trusting tsar. Indeed, it is curious that as soon as this circle became influential, it immediately concerned itself with its own princely patrimonies. Ivan the Terrible subsequently complained that his co-rulers, having taken all power from him, had reclaimed possession of towns and villages taken from the princes by his grandfather, and that they had permitted free transfer of princely lands taken under supervision by the Muscovite central power. Having once experienced the influence of princes whom he had incautiously taken into his confidence, Ivan the Terrible felt a sharp desire to free the sovereign's authority of all hindrance from the hereditary nobility: first, from their constant pretensions to precedence, and second, from the patrimonial estates still in princely hands. Ivan found the means for this in the *oprichnina* which he devised.

The essence of the *oprichnina* lay in the tsar's decision to apply to regions in which there were patrimonies of service princes that same policy of "deportation" which had been employed, as we have seen above, in Great Novgorod and, more generally, in lands subjugated by Muscovy. It was a well-tested device of assimilation by which the Muscovite state organism mastered new social elements, eradicating at the root the possibility of local separatism. This decisive means, originally intended for external foes, Ivan turned against internal "treason." He determined to remove the princes from their ancient patrimonial nests to new places, thereby severing their ties with local society and destroying their material prosperity.

Ivan did not bring about the "deportation" of the appanage aristocracy and the confiscation of its lands directly. He launched the policy in such an oblique way that it aroused general perplexity both among his own subjects and foreigners as well. He started by renouncing power and abandoning Moscow. This renunciation of power—an artifice, of course—he retracted upon the entreaty of the Muscovites, on the condition that no one thwart him in his struggle against treachery. He was to have the right "to impose disgrace on some and to execute others, and to seize their property and belongings, and to create in his realm an oprichnina: a special patrimony for himself and all his needs." This special court, with special boyars and gentry (a thousand *oprichniks*), towns and rural districts assigned to it, became the base for the entire operation of "deportation." Ivan systematically began to encompass in the oprichnina, within the jurisdiction of his new court, the lands which had made up old appanage Russia and in which the patrimonies of the princes were concentrated. On these lands the tsar "sorted through his servants," that is, the landowners. Some he "received" into his new oprichnina service, others he "sent away"—in other words, drove from their lands, giving them other lands on the periphery of the state (and instead of patrimonies, pomestie estates). In the course of twenty years (1565-1584) the oprichnina enveloped half the state and crushed the appanage seats of power by destroying princely landownership and by severing the ties of the appanage "sovereigns" with their patrimonial appanage territories.

Ivan's aim was achieved, but with consequences hardly necessary or beneficial. In place of the suppressed patrimonies of the princes, which had represented large economic units, there grew up petty, conditionally owned sections; moreover, a complex economic organization created by many generations of princely lords was destroyed. Peasant self-government, which had been alive on the large patrimonies, perished, and boyars' slaves were set free, exchanging the well-fed life of the boyar's household for a hungry and inhospitable freedom. The very essence of the instituted reform—the transformation of large-scale and privileged landholding into a small-scale form conditioned by service and obligations—must have aroused the discontent of the population. And the methods of introducing the reform provoked it even more. The reform was accompanied by terror. Denunciations, banishments, and executions of princes and other individuals suspected of "treason"; scandalous acts of violence by oprichniks against "traitors"; the bloodthirsty malice and debauchery of Ivan the Terrible himself—all this terrified and embittered the people. They saw in the oprichnina an incomprehensible and unnecessary terror, and did not understand its basic political aim, which the government had not openly explained.

Such was the notorious oprichnina of the Terrible Tsar. Directed against the aristocracy, it weighed upon the entire population; aimed at consolidating state unity and the supreme power, it shattered the social order and sowed general discontent. To be sure, the aristocracy was thereby broken up and dispersed, but its remnants did not react any better to the Muscovite dynasty, nor did they forget their proprietary traditions and pretensions. At the very moment of Ivan's death, before he had closed his eyes, Moscow was seething with open conflict over whether the oprichnina was to continue, while the princes who had been held under the tyrant's iron heel were already raising their heads and beginning to consider methods for regaining their power. Observing Moscow in the years right after Ivan the Terrible's death, the Englishman Giles Fletcher found that this "pollicy and tyrannous practise (though now it be ceassed) hath so troubled that countrey, and filled it so full of grudge and mortall hatred ever since, that it will not be quenched (as it seemeth now) till it burne againe into a civill flame." Thus the direct political consequences of the oprichnina made themselves felt; but it also had indirect consequences which influenced the development of a social crisis in the state.

2

This crisis was extremely complex. In general it stemmed from the conditions of life which were created in the sixteenth century as a result of the activities of the Muscovite government working under the pressure of military and political necessities. These resulted in wrenching away the agricultural and commercial-industrial labor force from the rural districts and towns of the Muscovite center.

As has already been mentioned, the Muscovite central authorities actively increased their armed forces, allocating pomestie estates to an ever greater number of servitors. They recruited them from all strata of the Muscovite population, transferring even privately owned slaves to state service and supplying them with pomestie estates. Only at the very end of the sixteenth century, when the number of servitors in the central regions had reached the desired level, did the thought arise that the state service ought to recruit with more discrimination, not including in the corps of *deti boyarskie* the "children of priests and muzhiks, or slaves of boyars and servants of monasteries." Formed from persons of the most varied social status, the class of servitors grew with extraordinary rapidity. Its economic maintenance demanded a vast expanse of land;

and these lands were allotted to it primarily in the southern and western parts of the state, according to proximity to the potential theater of war (with the Tatars, Lithuanians, and Swedes), and likewise around Moscow itself. In this entire expanse, service land tenure gradually attained an extremely high level of development in the sense that it came to embrace in its purview all land, except a part of the sovereign's own palace lands and church lands.

Under this system, of course, the "burdened" population everywhere found itself upon privately owned lands, and the free peasant commune disappeared. The communal-taxpaying structure of peasants could only be preserved where a large privately owned estate completely enveloped an ancient rural district, or where pomeshchiks found it to their advantage to preserve the self-government of the *"mir"* under their own supervision. The natural growth of pomestie landholding with its attendant peasant bondage was sharply complicated and accelerated by Ivan the Terrible's oprichnina. First, it extended the institution of pomestie landholding to the princely patrimonies, redistributing them in conditional tenure along with the remains of state "black lands," and thus it finally eradicated peasant self-government in the center of the state. And second, the oprichnina, operating through methods of ferocious terror, imparted to the agrarian reform the character of a social calamity which suddenly befalls and pitilessly ravages a country. The tales of contemporaries (the foreigners Taube and Kruse,[10] for example) about the liquidation of princely estates in the oprichnina startle us in depicting the malicious cruelty of that institution. That is why the 1570's witnessed, in close connection with the extension of the oprichnina's operations, the first symptoms of those economic con-

---

10. Captured by the Russians early in the Livonian War (1558-1583), the Livonian noblemen Johann Taube and Elert Kruse served in the Muscovite diplomatic corps and later defected to the king of Poland, Sigismund Augustus. They wrote an account of their Russian service in 1572. (T.)

sequences which led to the establishment of peasant bondage under the conditions of the system of pomestie landholding. These consequences were a mass peasant "departure" from the basic regions of the state to the borderlands and, as a direct consequence, the desolation of the center of the state.

3

This was the basic phenomenon in the economic life of the Muscovite State at that time. The laboring population of the center did not desire to remain in places where it was losing personal freedom and with it the former opportunity to use and to dispose of the land on which it lived and labored. It was as if the age-old thirst for new fields revived in the peasantry, and at the first opportunity peasant and slave left the boyar's household and the hated pomestie land, hardly thinking about the observance of the legal conditions of peasant "departure" or of slave release. The political situation of the time contributed much to such withdrawal; for Muscovite power was actively incorporating the conquests of Ivan the Terrible. On the broad expanses of the former Kazan khanate (to Muscovites, the "Lower Reaches") towns with large garrisons were being established, service landholders were being settled, and together with them monastic estates were being founded on new lands granted by the sovereign. These new landed estates needed peasant labor, while the new towns needed military and commercial-industrial personnel. Leaving their old nests in the regions of the upper Volga and Oka, peasants and slaves knew full well where they could go. The government itself summoned these emigrants from the Upper Reaches to settle the new towns and the fortified borderline in the Lower Reaches (along the Volga), and also on the "Wild Field" (to the south from the middle Oka in the black-soil zone). The new places enticed settlers with their wide-open spaces, attractive climate, and the riches of soil, forest, and river. Thus it happened that the central authorities by some measures, as it were, drove the oppressed populace out of the interior regions, and by others drew it to the borderlands which were attractive to settlers even without any government invitations.

The consequences of such a state of affairs soon became evident. A sharp crisis was created in the center of the state, provoked by a shortage of labor. The departure of the bulk of the labor force resulted in economic desolation. The land registers of the second half of the sixteenth century noted the many "empty clearings, which had been villages"; empty estates overgrown by the forest; settlements abandoned by the population, with churches without services; overgrown lands, uncultivated and deserted. In some places the memory of the departed cultivators still lived on, and the wastelands preserved their names; in other places even the lords were already forgotten, and "there is nobody to find their names."*

The small estates of petty servitors suffered most of all from the desolation. For the man who held a small pomestie estate there was nothing to sustain service and "nothing to collect in the future"; he himself went off to "wander between households," that is, to beg, abandoning his empty estate to the whim of fate. However, large landholders—both lay servitors and mon-

---

*Here are the figures for the district around Moscow in the years 1585-1586. In the thirteen sections of the district the land registers show up to 100,000 cheti of cultivated land [1 chet'=½ desiatina; 1 desiatina =2.7 acres]. Of this, up to 32,000 cheti were empty in pomestie and patrimonial estates and, in addition, 7,500 were leased out in the absence of owners. Hence, up to 40 per cent of the general amount of cultivated land had gone out of normal turnover. And the remaining 60 per cent was listed thus: for pomeshchiks 6 per cent (6,200 cheti), for hereditary owners 17 per cent (17,300 cheti), and for monasteries almost 37 per cent (36,800 cheti). This means that the servitors of the Moscow district by the end of the sixteenth century had left empty almost two-thirds of the total amount of arable land that they might have owned exclusive of monastery land; having kept 23,500 cheti for themselves, they had abandoned 39,500 cheti. The figures for the distribution of arable land in the Novgorod "fifths" in the years 1582-1584 lead to the approximate conclusion that of the general amount of land only 7.5 per cent was being tilled and that 92.5 per cent was empty.

asteries—enjoyed greater economic stability. They had the possibility of attracting peasants by the tax privileges which they enjoyed. The communal order of peasants preserved on their lands also bound the populace to them. Finally, it was not so easy to leave a large landholder, for he possessed all sorts of methods to overtake and return a runaway. The large estates not only kept their own working force, but persistently tried to transfer peasants and to indenture slaves from the outside, employing every kind of legal and illegal means toward this end. At that time the transfer of peasants from others' estates and similar forms of competition for labor assumed the character of a social calamity. On the customary days of peasant migration (around the St. George's Day in autumn) there unfolded a regular campaign of peasant "transportations." Some landowners took all measures, including open coercion, to prevent peasants from leaving their holdings; others used every means, even force, to gain peasants from other estates. The upshot of this struggle was that the poor and petty landowner lost out, while the richer and bigger landowners triumphed simply because they were economically more powerful.

The endless violence in this matter caused the government to become concerned. Under Ivan the Terrible certain measures, not exactly known to us, were adopted relating to peasant "transportation," and some sort of code was issued providing that peasants should not be taken away by force and that they might not leave at all at certain times—during so-called "forbidden years" which the government precisely defined in advance. The right of peasant "departure" was thereby temporarily abrogated. This abrogation already existed under Ivan the Terrible [in the early 1580's] and continued in effect to the very end of the sixteenth century; consequently, though it was acknowledged to be a temporary measure ("until a decree"), it continued to be applied and remained in force for entire decades. The suspension of peasant "transportation" aimed in general to fix the laboring population in place and to stop its mass exodus, and then to bind it to the small pomestie estates of military servitors and to curtail migration to large and privileged landholders, a process from which "great emaciation came to the military servitors."

4

The departure of the working population from the interior regions of the state was reflected not only in the abandonment of rural, cultivated estates and the households of hereditary owners and pomeshchiks. Towns became deserted as well, as the population of the commercial-industrial *posad*[11] left them. Study of the evidence by towns reveals a sad picture to the researcher. In the towns of Zamoskovie, around the capital itself and to the south of it, one observes an exodus of the population and its replacement by various service "ranks" in the urban posad, in the "burdened" households, and on the city square, "in the marketplace." The same necessities of national defense that had imposed the pomestie system upon the mass of the peasantry squeezed the laboring population out of the towns as well. The government maintained garrisons in them consisting of *"streltsy"*[12] and other ranks of "recruited people." In the leisure time from their service obligations these people engaged in industry and trade. Not bearing the burden of state taxes, they therefore enjoyed a tremendous advantage in commercial-industrial competition over those so "burdened." Furthermore, the gentry landowners of the district to which a town belonged were obligated to maintain, in case of enemy attack, their own "siege houses" in town, where they kept their own bondmen, "court people," who also took up trade and crafts. Finally, not in connection with the problem of town defense, privileged landowners—the boyars and the monasteries—added to the sovereign's posad their own

---

11. Posads were urban settlements with communal organization that paid taxes to the central government. (T.)

12. Literally "shooters," the *streltsy* were professional infantry armed with harquebuses. (T.)

private quarters [*slobody*], in which the people dependent upon them engaged in trade and handicrafts without paying the state taxes. In such circumstances the "burdened" posad commune in the towns of the Muscovite center was no longer master of its own posad or trade. Squeezed by the competition of newly arrived outsiders, both boyar and monastery servitors, the urban community abandoned its place of residence and wandered off in search of more favorable conditions for its labor. This process of the decomposition of urban taxpaying communes continued throughout the sixteenth century, resulting in the conversion of towns from centers of economic life into military-administrative points. It was as if the Muscovite town died a slow death; in its place a fortress grew up.

The only exceptions were those towns situated on the trade routes from the capital to the northern ports on the Murmansk peninsula and at the mouth of the Northern Dvina. The trade with the English and the Dutch that had sprung up in the middle of the sixteenth century at the maritime wharves of the North revived the commercial-industrial activity of those towns (Yaroslavl, Vologda, and others) which straddled the routes from the center of Muscovy to the White Sea and drew them into commercial circulation. Yet it was just this new factor in Russian economic life—the White Sea trade benefiting the Russian North—which dealt the decisive blow to the prosperity of Great Novgorod and its region. Under Muscovite rule Novgorod's commerce gradually declined—and not simply because Moscow had expropriated the boyars of Novgorod engaged in it. Muscovites had arrived to replace the local capitalists removed from Novgorod, and the central government was prepared to encourage them in every possible way in their new spheres of activity. Rather, the decay of Novgorod's trade cycle depended on international causes: on the decline of the Hanse and the growth of the Livonian towns, which sought by the crudest and most profitable methods to exploit the Russian market. They blocked access to the Baltic by Muscovite and Novgorodian merchants and did not allow the Russians "to trade there with those from beyond the sea without hindrance." Because of this persecution of Russian commerce and to obtain a free outlet to the sea, Ivan the Terrible had launched his Livonian War in 1558. But the protracted war [1558-1583] did not lead to success, and in the meantime it put an almost complete stop to commercial exchange on the western borders of Novgorod. The opportunity to enter into contacts with Europe via the northern route came just in time and, if one may say so, turned the face of commercial Muscovy from the West to the North for a long time to come. The northern trade routes and towns revived, and henceforth independently of military circumstances the western towns and trade routes began to decline. In the course of the second half of the sixteenth century Novgorod itself gradually fell into decay and lost its population. From 1546 through 1582 its population dropped from 5,000 households to 1,000; in other words, it lost up to 80 per cent of its inhabitants.*

The other towns and "fifths" of Novgorod Land also wasted away in the same manner. To the war and to the commercial paralysis provoked by the war other causes were also joined here. According to contemporary views, the region wasted away not only from war but also "from the tsar's exactions," "from the violence of the pomeshchik," "from a poor grain harvest," "from the oprichnina," and so forth. In the complexity of its destructive influences the depopulation of Novgorod Land clearly surpassed that of the other regions of the state and, in the words of N. F. Yanitsky, "by its proportions assumed the character of a terrible calamity." In a word, the entire territory of Novgorod was turned into a desert, and only at the very end of the sixteenth century are there perceptible in it any, however weak, signs of a revival of economic life and some increment of population.

---

*The latest researches (by A. M. Gnevushev, N. F. Yanitsky, and O. F. Tereshkevich) show that Novgorod wasted away in regular stages and that the well-known sack of the city by Ivan the Terrible in 1570 did not produce great desolation. The percentage of population loss in that year was no greater than in a series of adjacent years.

III

The population moves out of the basic regions to the borderlands.
1. The colonization of the Lower Reaches and of the Field and its peculiarities; the Cossacks.
2. The measures of the government for the defense and exploitation of the Field; the *desiatinnaia* land.

1

Muscovite governmental policy of the sixteenth century and the internal processes taking place in the Muscovite State had very curious consequences. Under Ivan the Terrible the territory of the state grew rapidly, expanding into the sparsely inhabited expanses of the lower Volga region and into the uninhabited "Wild Field" of the black-soil zone. The Lower Reaches of the Volga were acquired by conquest, the Field by private and governmental colonization. On the Lower Reaches lived non-Russian tribes—the Cheremis, Mordvinians, Votiaks, Bashkirs—who did not immediately recognize Muscovite authority and therefore required vigilant surveillance. The Field, in contrast, had no settled population, but was roved over by Tatar bands and Russian Cossack bands that had a common propensity for legal and illegal prey. In both areas Muscovite authority set up its fortresses to hold the restless local folk in submission and order. To institute this measure to the degree that was necessary for military purposes, the government summoned to the new regions immigrants from the interior and thus contributed to the mass migration and to the general depopulation of the center. The population flowed out to the borderlands and, destroying the economic organization in the old places of residence, created instead a new economy in their new home. Hence the government naturally faced the task of using the process which was taking place in the interests of the state.

The economic decline of the center deprived the government of revenues from the deserted lands and of service from the unprofitable and abandoned pomestie estates; it needed to obtain revenue and service from the new settlements. Hence the central authorities' concern to take appropriate measures in the new regions. On the Lower Reaches they strove to set up the very same forms of agricultural economy which existed in the center. This was because the Lower Reaches encompassed a settled non-Russian population that lived by various forms of agricultural labor, and on this local basis it was also easy to found both pomestie landholding and the privileged forms of hereditary holdings. The non-Russians' lands were distributed to pomeshchiks and granted to boyars and monasteries. In areas where the non-Russian working population was sparse, the authorities recommended "inviting" Russian laborer-colonists, migrants from the Upper Reaches. In such fashion Muscovite colonization of the Lower Reaches aimed to transplant there the old social forms.

It was a different situation as regards the Wild Field. Here there was no settled population; it ended in the Kaluga, Tula, and Riazan localities, while beyond them to the south in the first half of the sixteenth century, says a chronicler, "lay the field." There stretched out a wilderness without towns or villages, without cultivated land or agricultural plots, with only the temporary camps and the nomadic tents of hunters and fishermen. Until the middle of the sixteenth century the Tatars had held sway in this wilderness; their "Cossacks" had roamed about the limits of Russian settlement and had looted the Russian borderland [*ukraina*] with their raids. But in the middle of the century things changed; Russian Cossacks, who had come out onto the Field from the Muscovite State and from the Polish-Lithuanian borderlands, began to prevail. "At present, Sire, of Cossacks there are many—both of Cherkasses, and of Kievans, and of your own subjects on the field: they went out, Sire, onto the field from all the borderlands." Thus the *voevoda*[13] of Putivl reported in 1546. In various localities of the Field, Russian Cossack "townlets" appeared, and one of them—Razdory on the Don—served as a kind of center for the Cossack bands (that is, organized Cossack detachments) which roamed over the Field. At the head of the bands stood *atamen;* they gathered around themselves hundreds, even thousands of Cossacks and with them penetrated from the Don to the Volga, to the Caspian, to the Yaik (Ural). They waged a constant struggle against the Tatars and plundered everyone they found on the roads of the Field between Moscow, the Dnieper, and the Black Sea; but they also willingly hired themselves out for state service, constituting special detachments in the Muscovite armies, and they entered the service of private persons like Prince Mstislavsky in Venev and the Stroganovs on the Kama. The Russian Cossacks drove the Tatars from the Field and took both banks of the Volga away from them. Remaining outside the territorial limits of the state, the Field nevertheless became Russian, and its forests and the banks of its rivers hospitably welcomed fugitives from the center of the state. An unwritten but strict law of Field society prohibited agricultural labor there and threatened death to anyone who undertook cultivation of the land. On the Field it was only possible to live by some sort of hunting, whether of beast, fish, or man. Tilled land was viewed as a dangerous affair; you could not hide it from the Tatar or from the Muscovite official, and it brought with it captivity or bondage if seen by an unfriendly eye.

2

The Muscovite government took into account, of course, the extraordinarily rapid growth of Cossacks on the Field. It

13. Here, military governor; the term also meant simply general or commander. (T.)

was aware of the energy with which the laboring masses migrated there, fleeing from the interior regions of the state, and very soon it decided to exploit the colonization movement in order to bring the Field within the purview of the state. But the central authorities could not possibly deal with the Field as they had dealt with the Lower Reaches. On the Field there were no peasants; consequently, there could be neither patrimonies nor pomestie estates in their usual form. Here it was necessary to adapt to local conditions and to create new forms of society in accordance with the goals of the government. The needs of state defense dictated one series of arrangements within the limits of the Field, whereas the economic crisis in the center inspired another series of measures.

Defense needs demanded that the state's southern border be secured against the raids of the Crimean Tatars. From olden days this border had coincided with the course of the rivers Ugra and middle Oka and had seemed an impassable wall beyond which Tatar bands rarely sallied. Later, with the expansion of Russian settlement southward beyond the Oka, the border had shifted to the line of Tula and had been reinforced by all sorts of fortresses—wooden palisades, ditches and walls, blockhouses, and so on. The occupation of the Field by Russian Cossacks led to thoughts about the possibility and necessity of transferring all these fortresses as far south as possible, while the big Tatar raids of the 1570's forced the government to make haste in the matter. The authorities in Moscow systematically worked out a plan for the seizure of new stretches of the Field and shifted the fortified border from the Tula line to the river Bystraia Sosna, and then began to move it still farther south, using the course of the Oskol River. On the entire newly incorporated expanse, in places strategically important, fortified towns were established and between them, along a previously determined line, various forts were set out. In the towns garrisons were stationed, which were obligated not only to defend the town but also to keep watch over the entire line by sending out reconnaissance patrols. Thus sprang up dozens of the towns of the present-day black-soil belt between Tula, on the one side, and Belgorod and Valuiki, on the other. The whole area of the Field, where Cossacks had just established themselves, became enveloped by these towns. Beyond their boundaries and outside their influence remained only those Cossack bands which, huddled along the lower course of the Don, were accordingly called "Lower Cossacks." The remaining "Upper" Cossacks entered the sphere of government settlements on the Field and fell under the powerful influence of state authority. These Cossacks constituted a special form of service class under the general name of "recruited people" and under various specific names: atamen and service Cossacks, *streltsy*, cannoneers, guides, horsemen, and so on. In this way the Field was converted into a military border sector, and its population, having fled there to avoid personal bondage in its old home, fell under the yoke of the state in the new localities.

A town on the Field was usually built as follows. A Muscovite voevoda with a detachment of military and construction personnel arrived from the north at the site selected for the town, usually near a river, and built a fort. At the same time he gathered information from local sources about the free population and invited it to meet with him. He ordered "the atamen and the leading Cossacks from all the rivers to be with him in town." In the sovereign's name he made grants to them, that is, confirmed their holdings, "traditional possessions," as pomestie estates; he compiled a list of these landholders and enlisted them in state service to defend the town and the border. This was the first kernel of the service class conceived here: the petty pomestie-holding *deti boyarskie* or "service atamen"—pomeshchiks who did without peasant labor. A second kernel came from those garrison people whom the voevoda had brought with him for the construction of the town. Settled in the new town, this garrison served as the cadre from which the permanent groups of the urban population were gradually formed. In special suburbs around the fort settled service Cossacks, *streltsy*, and other military personnel—

each rank in its own suburb. These Cossack, *streltsy*, cannoneer, and other suburbs were assigned plow land near the town according to the number of their households. Gathered from the Field into a town and recruited into state service, the free wandering people settled down to a sedentary economy, and without returning "into the peasantry," they were nonetheless returned to the plow and the land. So, in the course of three or four decades the government succeeded, as it were, in overtaking on the Wild Field a large part of the population that had left the state, harnessing it to the yoke of service, and founding upon it a whole system of defensive measures against the Tatars. One can surmise that runaway people, who had been seeking land and liberty but who had unexpectedly fallen onto a state pomestie estate and plow land, were not satisfied with their new position. To be sure, here in the towns of the Borderland and the Field the old forms of pomestie and patrimonial modes of life were not reproduced. The various strata of servitors were not similar to the social classes of the center; there did not exist peasant bondage on small pomestie estates or household slaves on large patrimonies; but state service bound and indentured and, besides direct service, the state plow land oppressed as well.

This state, so-called *desiatinnaia*[14] land assumed special significance in the towns on the Field. It was one of the consequences of the economic crisis in the interior regions of the state. In a town's first years of existence on the Field its garrison was of necessity fed from grain brought from the north; but because of the shortage of grain in the center the authorities always hastened to cultivate land in the new localities to the greatest possible extent, and generously allotted to the garrison people large sections of arable around the town. Furthermore, in each southern district plow land was also instituted "for the sovereign," and the entire frontier population was enlisted for obligatory agricultural labor. They

---

14. From *desiatina,* a unit of measurement equal to about 2.7 acres. (T.)

cultivated the state *desiatinnaia* land with state-owned horses and tools, without any payment for their labor, and in quantities that were clearly beyond their abilities. Not having established yet their own economy in their new home, they overstrained themselves on the state land, the fruits of which did not accrue to them at all. The cultivators did not usually receive state grain; if it did not lie in the granaries as a dead reserve, it was sent farther south for the maintenance of servitors who did not yet have their own economy. At the end of the sixteenth century the grumbling of exhausted workers here and there forced the curtailment of the proportions of state arable. But in general it remained a misfortune for the population of the Borderland and the Field.

Muscovite policy in relation to the Field, as we have said, was prompted by motives of defense and was linked to the economic crisis of the center. Doubtless the Muscovite government, recognizing the heavy costs of the mass emigration to the central core of the state from the losses of people and revenues, aimed to recoup its resources by extracting them from the newly inhabited borderlands. The system of measures undertaken with such energy by Ivan the Terrible and his disciple Boris Godunov to colonize and to organize the borderlands was, of course, an attempt to find new sources of material means and working force in those regions to which the bulk of the labor force had spontaneously migrated from its old places of settlement.

IV

1. The results of the crisis and the premonition of Troubles.
2. The general course of development of the Troubles.

1

To review the results of the foregoing.

In the territorial composition of the Muscovite State at the end of the sixteenth century we have discerned five regions with distinctive characteristics in their social structure: the Muscovite center or Zamoskovie, the Novgorod "fifths," the Pomorie, the Lower Reaches, and the Field. The first two regions constituted the basic "halves" of the state and were experiencing a severe crisis. Politically the oprichnina had raged in them, and economically they were suffering utter ruin and desolation. The upper strata of the population had fallen victim to the executions and deportations of the sovereign, whereas the lower had fallen into bondage to the landowners—the pomeshchiks placed in the peasant rural districts. The apex of society had been shattered by the Wrathful Tsar, while the base was running away by itself, unable to endure its own misfortunes. In these regions it can be said that agriculture had died, while commercial exchange was paralyzed along the entire western border because of war and internal dislocations. The crisis did not touch the Pomorie, which had become a country of free peasantry after the removal of the Novgorod boyars. Its population in the sixteenth century had not yet broken down into mutually antagonistic groups, and it knew no other authorities than its own elected administration and the organs of central governmental supervision. With the opening of the White Sea trade the Pomorie came to life and began to grow rich from participation in the commercial exchange and transit of goods between the capital and the ports of Kola and Arkhangelsk. Centers of trade and commercial routes grew up in the Pomorie and helped to strengthen ties between the neighboring, previously dissociated, districts and lands into which the region was divided. In contrast to the center, for the Pomorie the sixteenth century was a golden era of the blossoming of its social forces and their independent activity. The Lower Reaches presented a special picture—a non-Russian land only recently conquered, pacified, and colonized by Russians. On the foundation of an alien mode of life and labor the usual forms of Muscovite society grew up there. The sharp contradictions between the Muscovite central authority and the aristocracy, between the Muscovite pomeshchik and the peasant, had not yet made themselves felt here; but a crisis of another kind was maturing—a struggle for land between the non-Russian natives and the newcomers who were imperiously seizing the landed wealth of the fruitful country. The Field also represented a special case, for the victims of the crisis fled hither in a great mass from the state—deprived people seeking freedom and good fortune in those places where the system of bondage did not yet exist. The Muscovite central authorities went into the Field after the runaways, surrounded them with towns, and instead of bondaged dependence, they created there a service dependence—military and agricultural. On the Field only those remained free who were not recruited as servitors and who went off farther south beyond the state's fortified frontier.

In the conditions of Muscovite life described above, perspicacious contemporaries saw a threat of open disturbances. They understood that the ruin which had befallen the center of the state, complicated by protracted war and governmental terror, could not pass without shocks. The aforementioned Englishman Giles Fletcher, in his account *Of the Russe Common Wealth,* printed in London in 1591, definitely predicted turmoil in the Muscovite State—revolution and civil strife as consequences of Ivan the Terrible's terror, which had aroused universal murmurings and irreconcilable enmity. He linked the beginning of the trouble with the end of the Muscovite dynasty, which he expected at the death of Tsar Feodor Ivanovich. As to the outcome of the turbulence, he said that in the confusion the decisive role—and therefore victory as well—would belong not to the aristocracy or to the mass of the populace, but to the social middle—to the army ("the militarie forces").

Such insight was not characteristic of Russians of the sixteenth century; yet they, too, had a foreboding of calamity. They even predicted upheavals, but only in the form of veiled hints and threats. Nevertheless, one of the anonymous writers of that time displayed remarkable foresight when he said that in Russia "at the end of time" districts and villages will be emptied, "without being persecuted by anybody"; "people will begin to leave everything, and the land will begin to be more empty, and there will be fewer people, and for the remaining people there will be no place to live on the empty land," and "the tsars will not be able to maintain themselves on their thrones and will be frequently changed." For observant persons it was clear, in short, that there could be neither peace nor prosperity in a country where whole regions were utterly ruined, where the hereditary aristocracy was oppressed and burned with hatred for the dynasty and its court favorites, where the service class was deprived of the possibility of service or proprietorship, where the lower classes were fleeing from dependence and from ruinous conditions of labor, and where, finally, the government had to rule in the absence of revenues and an army, amidst general discontent and grumbling. One can understand the fear felt by Muscovites, in the last years of the reign of the childless Tsar Feodor, as they awaited his death: his line would end with him, the "root" of Muscovite sovereigns would be severed, and turmoil would ensue.

This fear was well founded: upon the death of Tsar Feodor the Troubles commenced. The coincidence of disarray within the state with the end of the dynasty was the primary cause of the beginning of open disturbances. A powerful government could have struggled with the social movement and could have searched for a way out of the difficulties. But the government of the mentally incompetent Tsar Feodor was ill-suited for this. In it there was a man of major political talents —Boris Godunov—but he had to work amidst constant intrigues and extraordinary complications. The Troubles proved more powerful than Boris. They accompanied the beginning of his career, and they were the cause of his premature death and of the destruction of his family.

2

Thus, open disturbances in the Muscovite State began with the death of the childless Tsar Feodor Ivanovich in 1598. It is generally accepted that these ended with the accession to the throne of Tsar Mikhail Feodorovich Romanov in 1613. In this interval of time Muscovite life was filled with the struggle of diverse social and political forces. Looking closely at the course of this struggle, we note that at first the Muscovite throne serves as its object. For the possession of it contend various "seekers of power": the Romanovs against the Godunovs, then the Godunovs against the self-styled Tsarevich Dimitry Ivanovich, and in the end, after the pretender's death, the throne is held by a prince of the descendants of Rurik, Vasily Ivanovich Shuisky. This time (1598-1606) is the period of *dynastic confusion*.

Soon after the accession of Shuisky there ensues a series of uprisings against Tsar Vasily and against the "evil boyars" around him. Although the insurgents also clothe their activities in the name of Tsar Dimitry, whom they do not consider dead, it is nevertheless clear that the movement is no longer guided by dynastic motives but by motives of class antagonism. Against the slave-owning apex of society rise up the social depths—the Cossacks—bent upon a political and social revolution. This open civil strife lasts from 1606 through 1610 and can be called the time of *social struggle*.

Soon after the beginning of civil strife in Muscovy, all sorts of foreigners begin to interfere, seeking to exploit Muscovite weakness for their own private interests or for the benefit of their states—Sweden and the Polish Commonwealth [Poland-Lithuania]. This intervention leads to the transfer of the Novgorod and Smolensk border regions to the Swedes and to the Poles, respectively, while in Moscow itself, after the overthrow of Tsar Vasily, a Polish-Lithuanian garrison is installed. In such fashion the social confusion leads to the decomposition of the social order in the Muscovite State and to the collapse of national independence. The intervention of foreigners and their triumph over Muscovy arouses Russian national pride and turns all elements of the Muscovite population against the foreign enemies. In 1611 attempts to overthrow the alien power begin, but they cannot succeed so long as the blind irreconcilability of social classes undermines them. But when, in 1612, a military organization is formed in Yaroslavl which unites the middle classes of Muscovite society, the cause takes a different turn. The Yaroslavl provisional government succeeds both by inspiration and by force in influencing the bulk of the Cossacks to such a degree that it achieves the unification of all national forces, the restoration of the tsar's authority, and a unified government in the country. This period of the Troubles (1611-1613) can be designated the time of the *struggle for nationhood.*

The following exposition will be constructed according to the three periods indicated.

Chapter

THE
FIRST PERIOD
OF THE TROUBLES:
THE
DYNASTIC CONFUSION

I

The struggle of boyar circles for influence at court begins immediately upon the death of Ivan the Terrible.
1. The princely aristocracy and the court aristocracy.
2. Boris Feodorovich Godunov as regent; his political role.
2. The Godunovs and the Romanovs; the death of the Uglich prince, "Tsarevich" Dimitry.

1

The initial indications of the Time of Troubles appeared in Moscow in the very first days after the death of Ivan the Terrible. Ivan died on March 18, 1584, and on April 2 open disorder broke out on the central square of Moscow, *Pozhar* (or Red Square). An armed mob wanted to seize the entrance to the Kremlin and demanded the surrender of Ivan the Terrible's favorite, the oprichnik Bogdan Belsky, who, it was said, "wants to exterminate the tsar's line and the boyar families." The issue was whether to preserve the oprichnina under the successor of Ivan the Terrible, Tsar Feodor, or to abolish it. The populace supported the "boyars of the land,"[15] the princes Ivan Feodorovich Mstislavsky and Nikita Romanovich Yuriev, who were opponents of the oprichnina; they banished Belsky, who had almost been slain by the mob, from Moscow. Thus, at the outset a purely political question—concerning the system of internal government—was decided by the participation of

---

15. *Zemshchina,* i.e., that part of the country that had not been incorporated in the oprichnina and had retained the traditional forms of administration. (T.)

the mob. It was in response to its pressure that the hated oprichnina was abolished.

Such an intrusion of the mob into a quarrel among the boyars occurred because everyone in Moscow knew the qualities of Ivan the Terrible's successor, his son Feodor. Weak-minded and weak-willed, he needed guidance and guardianship, and the people wanted reliable persons around him. Mstislavsky and Nikita Romanovich Yuriev, especially the latter, enjoyed good reputations and popularity, and once they were in control the mob became peaceful. It was Nikita Romanovich who in fact ruled, since he was closest to the tsar, being his uncle by the female line. But when he fell ill in August, 1584, his place was taken by Tsar Feodor's brother-in-law, his wife Irina Feodorovna's brother, Boris Feodorovich Godunov. Both these rulers were so intelligent and shrewd that they were able to maintain order and obedience among the Muscovite population and did not themselves carry boyar intrigues or court secrets to the populace. Godunov even succeeded in bringing into submission the entire group of boyars, which was far from well disposed toward him. But, of course, he could not suppress those feelings of enmity and envy which his rapid and brilliant career aroused among the boyars. These feelings of the aristocracy for Boris personally became intertwined with the other motives of its discontent and created the basis for constant, though veiled, disturbances at court.

It has been shown above into what groups the ancient Muscovite aristocracy was divided. A distinction was made between "princely" families and the "age-old" group of untitled Muscovite servitors. Ivan the Terrible's oprichnina had smashed and humbled the princes and given the first places at court to the tsar's kin, who did not come from the princely group. Ivan had chosen no brides, for himself or his sons, from amongst the princesses of Muscovy. The tsar's brides were usually chosen from untitled families, and they brought with them to court and elevated representatives of the simple boyars or the gentry. This system formed at court a new aristocracy, in which the families of the Yurievs (earlier they were known as the Zakharins, later the Romanovs) and the Godunovs predominated. Around them were grouped their relatives and in-laws, among whom were also princes who were either intimates of, or related to, the powerful families of the court aristocracy. In opposition to this group the princely families, persecuted and intimidated by Ivan the Terrible, continued even after the oprichnina to constitute a special group of hereditary aristocracy, if not altogether removed from court, then set apart from its intimate life and outside the tsar's favor. In this group of boyars the princes Shuisky, Vorotynsky, Golitsyn, and Kurakin were most prominent. Their blood relations and relatives by marriage were representatives both of the powerful princely lines and of the simple boyars.

Thus, within the Muscovite aristocracy the ancient distinction between princely and non-princely lived on to the end of the sixteenth century; yet the character of this distinction changed somewhat. Both groups had sufficiently intermingled through marriages and other everyday intimacies to become variegated in composition. In the oprichnina epoch they had finally been equalized according to service position. But in one of them, the princely group, the old spirit still lived on. The traditions of the appanage period lingered on, as did their intense hatred both for the oprichnina, which had been aimed especially at this group, and for the dynasty that had traditionally oppressed the princes. In the non-princely group, however, fidelity to Moscow as the ancient place of service assumed the character of an attachment precisely to the dynasty, with which these people had succeeded in becoming related and in linking their own fate. Here, in contrast, reigned a desire to preserve the service and court order which had been created in the palace as a result of the oprichnina and the fall of the princes which it had caused.

At the moment of Ivan the Terrible's demise the princely group played no role at court, and the palace aristocracy ran affairs. Having eliminated Belsky and his design to preserve in unaltered form the oprichnina or "court" of Ivan the Terrible, Yuriev and Godunov did not, however, give free rein to the princes either. Having abolished the terrorist arrangements of the oprichnina that everyone hated, they nevertheless maintained the old tradition in regard to the princely families and thereby essentially continued the regime of Ivan the Terrible. Placed at the head of affairs, Boris Godunov seemed to embody personally this regime and therefore aroused against himself in particular the bad feelings of the boyar-princes. In their view it was necessary to eliminate him both as an overly youthful careerist and as the representative of a particular system. With his downfall the system itself might also topple, for with Nikita Romanovich's death Boris was the single able man left among the court aristocracy; its other representatives were either immature or insignificant.

In this combination of general and personal circumstances lay the cause of the plots against Boris Godunov undertaken by the high-born boyars in the first years of his rule. There were several such attempts, and Boris repulsed them all. As a result of clashes with him, his opponents disappeared from the palace and from Moscow: the aged Prince Mstislavsky wound up in a monastery, the princes Shuisky were exiled, Metropolitan Dionisy was removed from office, the Golovins were banished. . . . Boris overcame his enemies without terror or bloodshed. He executed only six or seven "muzhiks," who in 1587 provoked a street disturbance with the aim of requesting from "all the land" that the childless Tsar Feodor divorce Boris's sister and take another wife, "in order that the Tsar might have offspring." By inciting these muzhiks the princes Shuisky hoped that with Tsarina Irina's banishment Boris would also lose significance. Yet Boris contrived not only to exile the Shuiskys, but so strengthened himself in power that no intrigues frightened him. He arranged the matter in such a way that he became—formally and publicly—the regent of the state under the reality-evading Tsar Feodor, who was clearly incapable of ruling.

2

In the years 1588-1589 by a series of resolutions the Boyar Duma conferred on Boris, as "the brother-in-law of the tsar" and "wise ruler" of the state, the right of conducting foreign relations. From this time onward the splendid title gradually assumed by Boris took on practical significance: he actually became what the English had previously named him—ruler and regent ("livetenant of the empire" and "lord protector of Russia"). He "ruled the land at the hand of the great sovereign," for whom he publicly acted as guardian; he conducted the foreign policy of the Muscovite State, naming himself "majesty" on par with "His Majesty the Tsar" in Moscow and "His Majesty the Emperor" in Vienna. Like the tsar, he had his own court, where he maintained an etiquette similar to the order of the great palace. From an "intimate boyar," an "equerry," and a "servant," Boris was transformed into a magnate of such stature that he was "not a standard for anyone." It was officially said about him that "many tsars and tsareviches,[16] sons of kings and children of rulers serve the great sovereign (Feodor Ivanovich), but every tsar and tsarevich and king's son requests the love and kindness of the ruler from Boris Feodorovich. . . ." He was a great man, "brother-in-law to our sovereign, and brother to our great sovereign's wife." If one considers that while he was rising politically at court, Boris succeeded in concentrating in his own possession vast material means—land, revenues from leased landed properties, and remuneration from various offices—then it will be apparent how powerful he had become. He commanded everything needed for political domination. Court favor and influence, primacy within and power over the whole apparatus of government, exceptional wealth, and thousands of people dependent upon him as a landholder—all this put Boris beyond the danger of boyar competition and machinations. Who could openly oppose the guardian of the tsar and the head of the government?

---

16. That is, Tatar Khans and their sons. (T.)

But if Boris's position had been founded only upon his adroitness in palace intrigue it would not have been secure. To his deftness at court was joined a great talent for governing, generally recognized by his contemporaries. Boris was considered an exceptionally shrewd person, "a marvelous man of affairs," who in his personal qualities excelled the great multitude of men. He was not a bookishly educated dogmatist, was not even "versed in simple letters"; his strength lay in a practical mind and wisdom (*Weissheit und Verstande*, as one German who knew him expressed it), in a vast memory, in organizational skill and basic tact. Evidently he was by nature very kind, gentle, and hospitable: "sweet in answers to all," he loved to be charitable and to do good—"to those in need a giver generous." He stood up for those who were weak and who had been wronged: "against every evil repugnant to good, an avenger implacable." It is not surprising that he firmly wielded power, conducted a successful policy, and became popular: "thanks to such feats he is loved by all the people." In Moscow the people liked Boris very much; according to contemporary foreigners, "Boris so disposed them to himself that they talked of him everywhere." The middle classes, especially obligated to Boris for their prosperity, "looked on him as on God." "Having seen his prudence and justice," "just and firm rule," and "great affection for the people," the populace chose Boris to reign after Feodor Ivanovich died and his wife took the veil.

Boris's political role was very difficult, yet also respectable. The fate of the country was delivered into his hands in the hard days of a fateful crisis. The lost war for the Baltic littoral that had exhausted the state and ruined its western provinces; the dispersal of the population and the bankruptcy of landholding in the center; the terror of the oprichnina with its severe moral and material consequences—all this created a situation of exceptional difficulty. For about twelve years (1585-1597) Boris ruled the state under Tsar Feodor and had to dedicate all this time to struggling with the situation. He achieved great successes. In the sphere of foreign policy he forced Muscovy's neighbors—Sweden, Lithuania, and Poland—to recognize the rebirth of Muscovite political power after the defeats it had suffered under Ivan the Terrible. Under Boris's direction every facet of Muscovite political life, all of Muscovy's contacts with surrounding states, experienced an upsurge of governing energy and a recognition of its abilities and opportunities.

The tasks of the moment in internal policy were even more complex and more difficult than in foreign policy; but here, too, Boris was very successful. First, he unquestionably improved the general economic situation by his measures concerning commerce. Having lost the Baltic harbors because of war, Muscovy under Ivan the Terrible had ceased to trade with Europe and on the Polish-Lithuanian border as well; it had been left with only the northern trading route. Boris obtained some freedom of transit through Swedish lands for merchants coming from the Baltic with goods in the tsar's name. But since commerce in Narva remained exclusively in Swedish hands, Boris turned his whole attention to the White Sea trade and tried to organize it to the benefit of Muscovy, abolishing the exclusive privileges granted to the English trading company by Ivan the Terrible.

Second, while continuing the anti-princely policies of Ivan the Terrible, Boris completely altered the techniques of implementing them. He ended the terror and the cynical depravity of the "court" so closely associated with it. The Moscow palace became peaceful and moral; governmental techniques became gentle and technically skillful. The country breathed a sigh of relief. In the words of contemporaries, God "granted a happy time." Muscovites "from the sorrows of the past begin to comfort themselves, and to live quietly and serenely"; "brightly and joyously they are triumphant"; "from all blessings Russia flourishes." Thanks to such changes conditions in Muscovy noticeably improved; the population was calmed, even increased; commerce and every other economic activity revived and flourished. As a result it became possible to lessen somewhat the tax and service burdens imposed by the government on the population. Boris constantly pointed out that during his reign burdens were lightened, privileges were restored, freedom of choice was established at the marketplaces, the poor and the weak were given protection and every aid.

Yet these successes could not cure the principal ailment of Muscovite life. The crisis of landholding in the center persisted; pomestie lands remained without a working force; and the impoverishment of the service gentry was not decreased. The departure of the laboring populace to the borderlands did not lessen, and the struggle for working hands continued with great bitterness. Boris faced the urgent necessity of regulating the relationship of peasants and slaves to their lords and to the state. Moreover, he needed to clarify the attitude of the government to the antagonism between great and petty landowners, both in the peasant question and in the general sphere of land relationships, where large and privileged landholding was growing at the expense of the small pomestie estates.

In these complicated social conditions Boris followed a definite course: he kept in view, principally, the preservation of state interests, and in the class struggle he supported the side whose aspirations coincided with the government's goals. In general, the competition for land and peasants was leading to the ruin of small pomestie landholding, to the personal bondage of peasants, and to the development of slavery. All this was unprofitable for the government because it deprived the state of taxpayers and servitors. Boris took measures to support the petty pomestie-holding gentry, bound the peasant to them, and prohibited the transfer of the latter from small pomestie estates to large patrimonies. At the same time he opposed the conversion of peasants into slaves by means of advances and other methods of indenture. In all these cases governmental power upheld the small servitor and the "muzhik" against the large landowner, secular or ecclesiastical, and for its own purposes preserved the lower social strata from encroachments by the upper class upon their labor, their bondmen, and their lands.

This policy made Boris popular among the protected groups, but it did not yield rapid or certain results. The crisis was alleviated, perhaps, but not ended. The elemental antagonism of the landowning classes and the working masses could not be removed by governmental adroitness and wisdom alone.

3

Such, in the most general terms, was the governmental activity of Boris Godunov. At the beginning of 1598, at the moment of Tsar Feodor's death, he was indisputably the pre-eminent figure in the state, a popular ruler and illustrious philanthropist, whose "achievements on earth are such as never were: neither the great nor the powerful can offend anyone, not even the poor orphan." But, though "goodhearted by nature and charitable by temperament," Boris still had enemies. First among them must be counted, as has been said, the old hereditary princely aristocracy. They saw in Boris a pupil and disciple of Ivan the Terrible who, by the hated principle of the Muscovite dynasty, oppressed and humbled the eminent and established lesser families in their ranks with "undue haste and excess." Not only the princes thought so: foreigners, too, wrote that "Boris removed all the most eminent boyars and princes," and that the Godunovs were using every means to exterminate or to demean the most ancient aristocracy. The more firmly Boris wielded power, the more it spoiled his relations both with the newly formed aristocracy and with those boyar families which, like the Godunovs themselves, belonged to the group of palace favorites and relatives of the tsar.

In Boris's youth primacy among these relatives had belonged to that boyar clan in which each successive generation was called by the name and nickname of its grandfathers—the Koshkins, Zakharins, Yurievs, Romanovs. Especially distinguished among his kinsmen was Nikita Romanovich Yuriev, the brother of Tsarina Anastasia and celebrated "boyar of the land" under Ivan the Terrible. His reputation and popularity were such that he became the hero of folk songs. As we have seen, he had been the first guardian of Tsar Feodor and, until his illness, the chief personage at court. During his illness, apparently, he himself had yielded primacy to Boris, transferring to him not only guardianship over the tsar but also "supervision over his own offspring." The several sons of Nikita Romanovich were still too young to inherit immediately their father's leading position. Alliance with Boris was important to them, and evidently it was even made formal by kissing the cross; for contemporaries knew that Boris had "taken a terrible oath to them" to recognize the Romanovs as brothers and assistants in the governing of the state. Thus, both of the most eminent circles of the court aristocracy—the Romanovs and the Godunovs—had entered into a "sworn alliance of friendship" for the preservation of their own supremacy at court and, of course, for a possible struggle with the princely aristocracy.

But in the course of time this amity waned. The Romanovs grew up and began to envy Boris's power and glory. They considered their own family not lower but higher than the Godunovs, and no less than Boris they dreamed of the possibility of inheriting the throne from the childless Tsar Feodor. The young Romanovs were coming to personify Boris's most dangerous foe. Furthermore, the recollections which were still alive in Moscow of the meek "little dove," a wife of Ivan the Terrible, Anastasia Romanovna, and of her illustrious brother, Nikita Romanovich, surrounded the Romanov family with an aura of virtue and glory. The Godunovs had none of this aura, and Boris could counter it only with his personal reputation, which his enemies sought in every way to malign.

At that time a circumstance existed in Muscovite life that could be used against Boris. It was the death of the so-called "Tsarevich Dimitry," the younger half-brother of Tsar Feodor, born to Ivan the Terrible by his seventh wife, Maria Nagoi. The canonically illegal marriage made the fruit of this union of doubtful legitimacy. After his father's death, however, the baby Prince Dimitry—he was then so entitled—was acknowledged appanage prince of Uglich and sent there "on appanage," together with his mother and uncles. To be sure, by this time an "appanage" was already a fiction, and at Uglich alongside the appanage court resided and functioned agents of the central government, both regular Muscovite officials (the state secretary [*d'iak*], Mikhail Bitiagovsky) and temporary ones (the town prefect, Rusin Rakov). Between the Nagois and these representatives of governmental authority there was constant antagonism, because the Nagois would not renounce the dream of appanage autonomy and held that the Muscovite government and its agents were violating the rights of an appanage prince. The central authorities, of course, were not disposed to countenance appanage pretensions and constantly gave the Nagois pretexts for resentment. In such a situation of constant spite, abuse, and quarreling, young Dimitry perished.

On May 15, 1591, Dimitry died of a wound in the throat, inflicted by a knife while playing blocks with buffoons in the inner court of the Uglich palace. Eyewitnesses to the event later told the official investigators, Prince Vasily Ivanovich Shuisky and Metropolitan Gelasy, that the tsarevich had stabbed himself in a sudden attack of "falling weakness" (more precisely, during an epileptic seizure). But at the moment of the incident Dimitry's mother, beside herself from grief, began to scream that the tsarevich had been stabbed. She suspected the Muscovite official Bitiagovsky and his fellows. Summoned by a tocsin, the crowd staged a massacre. Bitiagovsky's house and chancery ("prefect's office") were ransacked and more than ten persons were killed. After a thorough investigation the Muscovite authorities declared that the tsarevich had perished by accidental suicide, that the Nagois were guilty of incitement to riot and the Uglichans of murder and pillage. The guilty were exiled to various places, "Tsarina" Maria Nagoi was confined as a nun in a distant monastery, and the tsarevich was buried in the Uglich cathedral. The body was not taken to Moscow, where members of the grand princes' or tsars' families were customarily buried—"in the Archangel [cathedral] with the most illustrious forebears of the tsar." Furthermore, Tsar Feodor did not go to his brother's funeral; and, far from becoming a shrine, the grave of the tsarevich was so inconspicuously marked that it could not immediately be found when a search for it was made in 1606.

It came to this: nobody in Moscow mourned the tsarevich; on the contrary, they tried to forget him. But it was all the easier to spread dark rumors on the occasion of this extraordinary affair. It was rumored that the tsarevich had been murdered, that his death had been necessary to Boris, who wanted to reign after Tsar Feodor, and that Boris at first had sent poison to the tsarevich and then had ordered him stabbed when the youngster was saved from the poison. Simultaneously there was talk that in case of Feodor's death the throne must not go to Boris, but to the eldest of the Romanovs, whose family was more eminent than the Godunovs. Although no one in Moscow said that the Rurikovich princes had a better right than others to the throne, persons in Poland were quite certain that by right of princely primogeniture the princes Shuisky ought to be considered the successors to the extinct Muscovite dynasty.

All such talk was premature. It was difficult to say that Tsar Feodor was "offspringless," for his spouse was not unfruitful: she bore dead children. But in 1592—after the death of Tsarevich Dimitry—a live daughter was born, the Tsarevna Feodosia.[17] Boris knew, of course, that the "tsar's seed" might still "blossom" from Tsar Feodor, and that the murder of an illegitimate half-brother of the tsar would not necessarily open the road to the throne. It would seem that from these considerations alone Boris could not have become a thoughtless murderer. But besides these considerations he could not have had, in the days of the tsarevich's death in 1591, any special fear of Dimitry's political emergence. In the expectation of posterity the tsar, in order to guarantee the future of his beloved wife,

17. She died the very next year, however. (T.)

had formally made her co-ruler in affairs of state. For the first time in Muscovite governmental practice the tsarina, as the first adviser to her spouse, took part in the discussion of state and even church affairs on a par with the boyars. This practice gradually prepared the transfer of the tsardom to Tsarina Irina, who would accede upon the death of Tsar Feodor. If the appanage prince Dimitry had remained alive, his right to the royal succession would have been contested by Irina. As the lawful wife and long-time co-ruler with the tsar, Irina would have had, it stands to reason, a much better right to the throne than an illegitimate, epileptic tsarevich from an appanage. To be convinced of this, one need only recall the merciless, contemptuous severity with which the old Russian legal mind regarded illegitimate children, officially designating them by an unprintable word (see the Law Code of 1649: ch. X, art. 280). Boris the ruler made his own sister, Tsarina Irina, co-ruler of the doleful tsar. This very step defeated Dimitry more surely than poison or knife, since it prepared his political death; hence Boris had no need to kill him physically. However, gossip against Boris implanted itself in unsophisticated and malicious minds and, without rising to an exact understanding of the situation, gave him the reputation of a lover of power, who for the sake of power and the tsar's mantle was even capable of a bloody crime.

II

Open struggle for the throne begins with the death of Tsar Feodor Ivanovich.
1. The election campaign of 1598; the triumph of Boris and the fall of the Romanovs.
2. The pretender: his appearance and probable origin.

3. The campaign of the pretender against Moscow.

4. The death of Boris and the fall of the Godunovs.

5. The rule of the pretender and his overthrow; the role of Prince Vasily Ivanovich Shuisky.

1

Such were the circumstances of Muscovite court life when Tsar Feodor died. Toward morning on January 7, 1598, "the light of the Russian land was extinguished, the candle of Orthodoxy went dark." Tsar Feodor suffered an "incursion of the cloud of death" and, departing into the life eternal, left the realm temporal to his wife Tsarina Irina. The court and the city of Moscow swore allegiance to their sovereign and thereby completed Irina's accession. However, Irina did not wish to remain in power, even though she was requested to order her brother Boris to rule while herself remaining grand sovereign in name only. She left for a monastery and took the veil. And only then did the Muscovite throne become "widowed," and Muscovy became "sovereignless." By the tsarina's decree provisional power passed to Patriarch Iov, and the boyars had to "report affairs" to him. Upon the patriarch lay the responsibility of arranging for the election of a tsar. The patriarch put off this matter until the fortieth day of the late tsar's decease (February 15, 1598). On that day he set a meeting of the *Zemsky Sobor,* [18] inviting to it all those who "habitually attend great Sobors." At the same time he ordered the Muscovite people, "who are in Moscow," to "consider among themselves generally who will be their sovereign." In other words, he opened pre-election meetings in the capital for the preliminary discussion of the matter and preparation of the Sobor.

18. Assembly of the Land, a kind of Muscovite estates-general. (T.)

The composition of the Sobor which convened on the date fixed by the patriarch is known. It has been investigated by V. O. Kliuchevsky and declared proper for the sixteenth century according to the system of representation then obtaining. Its membership included: nearly 100 ecclesiastics; about 50 boyars and other members of the Duma; up to 300 service gentry; about 36 "burdened" people from commerce and industry. The formalities of the electoral procedure were irreproachable: the Sobor was legal and proper; its leader, the patriarch, was acting by authority of the tsarina; discussion of the question in private gatherings had preceded the Sobor itself. If there was any kind of agitation or struggle among candidates for power, it did not distort the composition of the Sobor and did not make it a farce. The matter proceeded in orderly fashion.

At its very first general session on February 17 the Sobor elected as tsar Boris Godunov, after a speech by the patriarch in which he declared that the gatherings which had preceded the Sobor had all arrived at the decision "not to seek or to want any sovereign" besides Boris. Without debate the Sobor associated itself with the patriarch's thinking and consequently only sanctioned a previously resolved decision. Since Boris and Irina did not immediately submit to its election, the Sobor discussed in the following days measures by which it might influence their will. It was decided to organize a sacred procession to the Novodevichy Monastery, where Boris was staying with his sister; on February 21 the Zemsky Sobor was to lead out the entire populace of Moscow with the holy icons to plead with Boris. This celebrated sacred procession, more than once described by historians, achieved its aim. Boris agreed to become tsar, and Irina blessed him with the tsardom.

Thus official documents depict the course of the election; thus a chronicle of the seventeenth century recounts the election of Boris. But many private reports of contemporaries circumvented this external, parade side of the matter and pointed to what allegedly had been going on backstage. According to these accounts, Boris took all precautions to insure that precisely he would be asked to the throne. Some people he courted, others he threatened; his agents were active everywhere. The sacred procession of February 21 was organized with the aid of Muscovite police obedient to Godunov; they drove the Muscovites by force to the monastery and forced them by beatings to cry out and request Boris. There was allegedly no legality, no justice, and not the slightest propriety in the manner whereby Boris took possession of the throne. One of the Russian writers of that epoch who belonged to the camp of the princes Shuisky says, in describing the machinations of Boris, that he succeeded by guile in deceiving the aristocracy: "the great boyars, both from the branch of the scepter-wielders (i.e., the princes Shuisky) and from the kin of the great sovereign Tsar and Grand Prince Feodor Ivanovich of All Russia (i.e., the Romanovs), and those worthy of election as tsar, did not want to act at all or to choose among themselves, but left it to the will of the people." It was as if they believed in the love of the populace for Boris, which the latter had so deftly and unscrupulously staged. From the foreigners living in Moscow at the time who have left accounts we find the same reports about the crude and cunning influence of Boris on the popular will, about the farce of the election.

Reading similar accounts, we feel ourselves in the realm of common gossip, in which it is not easy to tell a lie from the truth and the serious from the ridiculous. More important than all such gossip are the regular reports of the Lithuanian frontier commander, the governor of the district of Orsha, Andrzej Sapieha.[19] During the election campaign of 1598 he tried to collect for his government exact information about Muscovite affairs and directed his spies to the nearest Muscovite city, Smolensk. Everything they sent back to him he passed on to the authorities in Lithuania. These crucial communi-

19. In Russian the name of this family is spelled Sapega or Sopega. (T.)

cations, which have come down to us, are especially curious and important.

Sapieha learned that after Feodor's death Irina had ascended the throne, that she did not remain in power but had renounced the world and entered a monastery, and that in Moscow four candidates for the tsardom had immediately appeared: Feodor Nikitich Romanov, Boris Feodorovich Godunov, Prince Feodor Ivanovich Mstislavsky, and Bogdan Yakovlevich Belsky. The last two were not serious claimants, and the contest was between Romanov and Godunov. At first it seemed to Sapieha that Romanov had the better chance: it was alleged that Tsar Feodor himself had considered him a possible successor. So far as Godunov was concerned, he was, allegedly, accused of murdering Prince Dimitry, so that Feodor Romanov even wanted to kill him himself, but was restrained by others when he rushed at Boris with a knife. In Sapieha's eyes Boris's chances gradually grew. He learned that the Muscovite *streltsy* and the common people were on Boris's side, whereas several circles of the boyars wanted Romanov. More than once Sapieha remarked that the election struggle in Moscow was acute, that it threatened bloodshed, and that it fostered social commotion. Curiously enough, this intelligence from Sapieha is confirmed by German letters of the same time sent from Pskov to Germany. In them it was reported that Boris had not acceded to the throne smoothly, that there was great confusion in Moscow stemming from the tsar's election, and that the grandees did not want to reconcile themselves to the election of Boris. All this information throws a bright light on Boris's accession.

It turns out that the tendentious account of Godunov's bitter Muscovite enemies is completely false in its description of the state of affairs. Neither the boyars nor the populace were passive victims of the threats and bribery of a lover of power. Representatives of the two principal families of the court aristocracy—the Romanovs and the Godunovs—grappled for the Muscovite throne in an embittered and open contest. The princely aristocracy remained to the side of the melee. Prior to the Sobor of February 17, 1598, Moscow was deciding amidst protracted confusion the question of the person of the future tsar and was weighing the chances of the candidates. By the day of the Sobor the matter had been decided in favor of Boris, and at the Sobor it was formulated by "unanimous" election. There are indications that even after the Sobor the opponents of the Godunovs did not want to reconcile themselves to his success and hoped to keep Boris from the throne. Sapieha heard a rumor that in the spring of 1598 the Romanovs and Belsky had attempted to replace Boris with another person— namely, with the Tatar "Tsar" Simeon Bekbulatovich, who under Ivan the Terrible had borne the title of "Grand Prince of All Russia." But this little intrigue (or even plot) did not succeed, and Boris was crowned tsar on September 1, 1598. He took the very first occasion to secure himself in the future against his rivals and bitter enemies. At the end of the year 1600 he succeeded in obtaining some evidence against Belsky and the Romanovs and brought them to trial. The investigation and trial found guilty (or, more precisely, accused) of a design against the sovereign's person the entire Romanov family and the related families of the princes Cherkassky, Sitsky, Repnin, Shestunov, and others. All of these persons, Belsky included, were exiled to remote places, while the elder Romanov, that same Feodor Nikitich who had contested the throne with Boris, was tonsured as a monk—in other words, suffered political death. The crushing defeat of the Romanov clique represented the last act of the election battle, after which, it seemed, Boris could consider himself secure on the throne.

His position, however, was very delicate. No one could oppose him openly; his popularity with the bulk of the populace was undiminished, and his authority was firm. Nevertheless, he could not help but feel his own political isolation, in which he found himself from the time of his accession. Before his election to the tsardom Boris had been recognized under Tsar Feodor as the head and leader of the court aristocracy, which was united with him by a sworn alliance of friendship against the other segment of the Muscovite aristocracy—the princes. Election to the tsardom had embroiled him with friends who, like himself, were seeking the throne. In the heat of the struggle he had smashed them and, by throwing the Romanovs and their kin out of Moscow, had in reality destroyed the entire old court circle. The Godunovs, having turned themselves into a dynasty, remained the sole representatives of the former court aristocracy. The princely aristocracy was hostile to the Godunovs. The "elder brethren" among the princes—the Shuiskys, Vorotynskys, Golitsyns, Kurakins—did not have the strength to contend with the Godunovs for the throne, for they were oppressed and kept in the background. But neither could they rejoice over the accession of Boris; they considered him, of course, a usurper of their rights, a persecutor and an oppressor. Under such circumstances the Godunovs were completely isolated; they had to beware of all, to suspect all, to spy on all. This explains the existence of the system of denunciations and petty investigation which flourished during the reign of Boris and which in the hands of Semen Nikitich Godunov was turned into a terrible and hated instrument of the tsar's protection. Sensing his own isolation and the absence of a sympathetic and compatible governing class about him, Boris could not help but understand that he alone bore the entire burden of power; for among his relatives there was not one eminent figure who could be an assistant and replacement for him, while among the courtiers there was no cohesive circle of men in whom he might trust and upon whom he might lean for support.

2

So the Godunovs were in power with a circle of their own kin; the Romanov circle was destroyed; the princely aristocracy was oppressed. All affairs of state were in the adroit hands of Tsar Boris, and he had no further rivals. Such was the general situation in Moscow at the very turn of the sixteenth and seventeenth centuries. Just at this moment of complete and undivided triumph for Boris his vanquished enemies succeeded in laying the foundation of the Godunovs' ruin. They created the self-styled Uglich prince "Tsarevich Dimitry," claiming that he was the legitimate son of Tsar Ivan the Terrible and alleging that he had the right to inherit the "patrimonial throne." At the very moment of the tsar's election in 1598 the accusation was thrown in Godunov's face that he had ordered the murder of Prince Dimitry, and that he had an "acquaintance" or "friend" resembling Dimitry who was ready to masquerade for the deceased if Boris should need to resurrect the tsarevich. Rumor had it that Feodor Romanov had suggested this accusation against Boris. Whether this is true or not makes no difference: in 1598 this strange accusation existed and was circulated to such an extent that it migrated into Lithuania and there became known to Andrzej Sapieha.

It was impossible, of course, to explain why Boris might need a pretended Dimitry, but he was necessary to Boris's foes: only with a legitimate son of Ivan the Terrible would it be possible to overthrow Boris and to destroy him. Dimitry was not resurrected in the days of the tsar's election in 1598, but in 1600 a rumor floated about Moscow that he was alive and had gone abroad. The affair of Belsky and the Romanovs, from whom Boris thought to expose the root of the pretender intrigue, had apparently originated in connection with this rumor. What he found out from them is not known, but the exile of Belsky and the Romanovs failed to stop the intrigue. In 1603 definite news arrived from the Polish Commonwealth about a person there naming himself Tsarevich Dimitry Ivanovich, the son of Ivan the Terrible saved from an attempt on his life by Boris Godunov. This person was recognized by the Polish government as the authentic tsarevich, despite Moscow's official declaration that he was an impostor and really the monk Grigory Otrepiev. In March, 1604, there took place a final *rapprochement* between the impostor and the Jesuits, and on April 24 he became a Catholic and himself informed Pope Clement VIII of his conversion via a solemn letter in Polish. From this moment began, so to speak, the official existence of a claimant to the Muscovite throne, and Boris had to anticipate incursions on the borders of his tsardom by an armed foe.*

Of all extant opinions as to the origin of the pretender the most probable is that he was Muscovite, groomed for his role by the group of Muscovite boyars hostile to Godunov and sent by them to Poland. At least his letter to the Pope testifies clearly that it was written not by a Pole (though composed in excellent Polish) but by a Muscovite who poorly understood the handwriting which he had to copy from a rough draft in Polish, obligingly prepared for him by the Jesuits. In vain shall we seek in Poland or Lithuania for a group of persons to whom we might attribute the initiative in the design and preparation of the Muscovite tsarevich. Contemporaries testify that Boris himself, as soon as he heard about the appearance of the pretender, immediately said "to the princes and boyars in person" that it was their doing. Evidently, the investigation undertaken by Boris convinced him that the pretender's role had been assumed by the monk Grigory Otrepiev, and he did not hesitate to inform the Polish government of that fact. Of course, he might easily have accused the Poles not only of harboring the impostor but of actually substituting the person who had assumed the name of Dimitry. By not making this accusation against the Poles, Boris thereby gave grounds for seeking in Moscow those guilty of the intrigue. He himself obviously suspected the roots of the plot among the families of the Romanov circle.

---

*There is no need to relate here the previously known details of the appearance of the pretender in Poland and his personal adventures before his campaign on Moscow. Those interested can read about this in the works of Father Paul Pierling, S.J., especially in his book, *La Russie et le Saint-Siège: Études diplomatiques*, Vol. III (Paris, 1901); Russian translation by V. P. Potemkin (Moscow, 1912).

Some circumstances point to this. In 1605, when informing the populace of the war with the pretender, Boris's government announced that the impostor was named Grishka Otrepiev and that he had lived in the household of the Romanovs. A little later, immediately after the overthrow of the pretender, a Muscovite embassy to Poland officially announced that the deposed Grishka had been a "slave of the boyars, of the children of Nikita Romanovich and of the Prince Boris Cherkassky, and having committed an offense, was shriven as a monk." This statement repeated, in essence, the version that Moscow under Boris had officially communicated to Emperor Rudolf II in Vienna at the end of 1604—that Grishka had been in the service of Mikhail Nikitich Romanov. Private accounts also testified that Otrepiev had been connected with the household of the Romanovs and the Cherkasskys. One such tale asserted, in direct connection with the affair of the Romanovs and Cherkasskys, that Grishka had "concealed himself" from Boris in a monastery because he "frequently came to the rich house" of Prince Boris Cherkassky "and from Prince Ivan Borisovich obtained honor, and for this reason Tsar Boris is indignant with him." Actually, Prince Ivan Borisovich Cherkassky, a close relative of the Romanovs, was among those most suspected in the plot of the Romanovs, just as subsequently he was among those grandees closest to the impostor. In connection with this private account about the "honor" shown Otrepiev in the Cherkassky household, the incidental but important evidence of Margeret[20] (who believed in the authenticity of the self-styled Tsar Dimitry) gains weight, since he says that the Romanovs were among those grandees who had saved the

---

20. Jacques Margeret, a French soldier of fortune, entered Muscovite service in 1601 and under Boris Godunov commanded a squadron of foreign cavalry. He served the pretender but escaped death in the massacre of 1606, soon afterward leaving the country. Later he returned to Moscow in 1611 in Polish service. His memoirs, an important source for the period, are entitled *Estat de l'Empire Russie, et Grand Duché de Moscovie avec ce qui s'y est passé de plus memorable et tragique, depuis l'an 1590 jusques en l'an 1606* (Paris, 1607; 2nd ed., 1669). (T.)

youngster Dimitry from destruction at Uglich. Thus, several hints bring the researcher to the same suspicion that Boris had reached in his own time: namely, that the roots of the pretender intrigue were hidden somewhere in the depths of the court aristocracy hostile to Boris, and most probably in the circle of the Romanovs and their kin by blood and by marriage. When the forces of the pretender appeared on the Muscovite borders and it became necessary to send a Muscovite force against them, Boris without hesitation entrusted its command to the hereditary princes: Trubetskoi, Mstislavsky, Shuisky, and Golitsyn. He did not fear their betrayal or defection, for he knew that this blue-blooded group was far removed from the pretender plot. And he was not mistaken: these princes drove the impostor into Putivl and only by chance failed to destroy him. But in his army Boris did not send any of those connected with the Romanov circle who had escaped disgrace or exile, in accordance with their manifest unreliability and vacillating attitude toward him. Nor do we see in the military command of the forces operating against the pretender anyone from the families involved in the plot of the Romanovs. Boris could assume that the Romanov group included those of his enemies who desired the impostor's success and about whom a contemporary remarked: "they rejoiced at his (the pretender's) approach to Moscow, and when they heard of victory over the Muscovite forces of Boris, they did rejoice; but when they heard of victory over the expected Dimitry moving toward Moscow, then shaken and depressed they went about with downcast eyes."

The personal behavior of "elder" (that is, monk) Filaret Romanov at the time of the pretender's appearance on the Muscovite borders provides some indication of the mood of Boris's enemies. It is curious to compare two reports about the "state traitor" elder Filaret by his guards—one in November, 1602, the other in February, 1605. In the first the guard reported the complete collapse of Filaret's spirits: he desired death for himself and his wife and children. "My dear little children," he lamented, "are left small and poor . . . evil for me are a wife and children: when you remember them, something pierces the heart like a horn! . . . Grant, O Lord, that God shall take them early!"

Two years passed. The Siisky Monastery where Filaret was held captive was visited by people both in winter and in summer: "trading people of those towns came by road to pray," and other people came "from other towns" to live in the monastery. With these travelers news of secular affairs reached the monastery brotherhood and the prisoner Filaret about the resurrected Dimitry and the civil war in the state. And the prisoner revived at the beginning of 1605. "Elder Filaret does not live according to the monastery rule," his guard reported to Moscow; "he always laughs for no reason and talks about secular life, about falcons and hounds, and about how he lived in the world; and to the elders he is cruel." Filaret threatened the monks with everything; they constantly complained that he "howls at them and wants to strike them." He even "ran at one of them with a crozier"; "and the elder Filaret says to the elders: they will see what he will be in the future." Hope for freedom and for life outside had seized hold of Filaret; the monastery administration itself was influenced by his mood, weakened its supervision over him, and departed from its previous solicitude. So it was in February, 1605. In the summer of that year Filaret had already received his freedom from that same pretender whose first appearance had filled him with bright hopes.

3

Thus, the struggle for the throne and for power between the Muscovite "seekers of power" developed a new aspect—it gave birth to the self-styled Dimitry. He appeared in the Russian districts of Poland in the latter half of 1603 as a prepared claimant to the Muscovite throne. He had received the attention and support of both secular and clerical politicians in Poland. The dynastic struggle and confusion in the Muscovite State, which had firmly established itself again after recent defeats, played into the hands of the Polish government; it was therefore ready to aid Dimitry within the limits of international propriety: not entirely openly and not completely officially. At that time clerical circles in Poland were interested in the possibility of uniting with Muscovy or even converting it to Catholicism in the interests of a general European coalition against the Turks and the Tatars. In the name of this utopia they seized upon the Muscovite "Tsarevich" and hurriedly converted him to Catholicism, believing that a Catholic tsar might bring his entire tsardom into the bosom of the papal church. Thanks to the lofty patronage of the authorities and to the cooperation of the clergy, the pretender received the opportunity to prepare publicly for a campaign on Moscow. Having established himself at the magnate Mniszech's Sambor castle, he recruited an army and collected funds. Around him gathered the most varied people: the native Muscovite, and right with him the Polish noble who scorned everything Muscovite; the "peasant-brigand" who had fled Muscovite bondage, and with him the petty noble servitor who represented the support of that same bondage; the punctilious "knight" of free Poland, imbued with military honor and all the conventions of his time and class, and with him the Cossack of the steppe who knew no conventions and thirsted for booty alone—such were the men who rallied to the pretender under a single banner and command. Rabble of this sort did not promise the impostor great successes, even if his army had been large. But there is evidence to suggest that his force did not exceed 3,500 or 4,000 men, and therefore contemporaries said that the "tsarevich's" incursion into the Muscovite State was not like a serious hostile invasion. The pretender led only a handful of people and "from only one corner of the Borderland advanced to the Seversk border."

Yet the pretender's own army did not constitute his principal source of strength. From the very start of his activity in Poland he was in contact with the population of the Muscovite Borderland and the Field. His "seductive letters" (proclamations) were distributed over the Muscovite South by many methods: they were carried across the border in sacks of grain; they were hidden in boats. In response to these "secret sheets," messengers on foot and Cossacks from the Don came out of the Muscovite State to the impostor, and after calling on the "true Tsarevich," they went back and raised the populace against Tsar Boris. When the pretender's motley army crossed the Muscovite borders on the banks of the Dnieper and the Desna, hundreds and thousands began to join him, and by the time he reached Chernigov he had, it was said, as many as 10,000 Cossacks. In addition, separate from Dimitry's own army, to the east of him on the roads from the Wild Field to Moscow, a special Cossack and servitor force assembled, operating in the name of Dimitry and to his advantage. In such fashion, one can say that the pretender and his agents and inspirers launched their struggle with Boris by organizing against the Muscovite government a revolt of the southern regions of the state. It was just this revolt that led to victory for the invaders.

The soil upon which this uprising could develop is already familiar to us. We have seen the conditions of the settlement of the Field. Dissatisfied with government policies, the bulk of the population had filled the "edge of the Muscovite land" with "belligerent people" of an oppositionist tendency. Rapid governmental colonization of the Field had overtaken these people in their new places of settlement, surrounded them with forts, recruited them into state service, and put them on the land. Yet besides their own arable sections, they had to till the burdensome state *desiatinnaia* land. Thus the state regime, from which the population had fled "unable to bear it," overtook the fugitives and oppressed them anew. In this fact lay the cause of the constant irritation and profound dissatisfaction

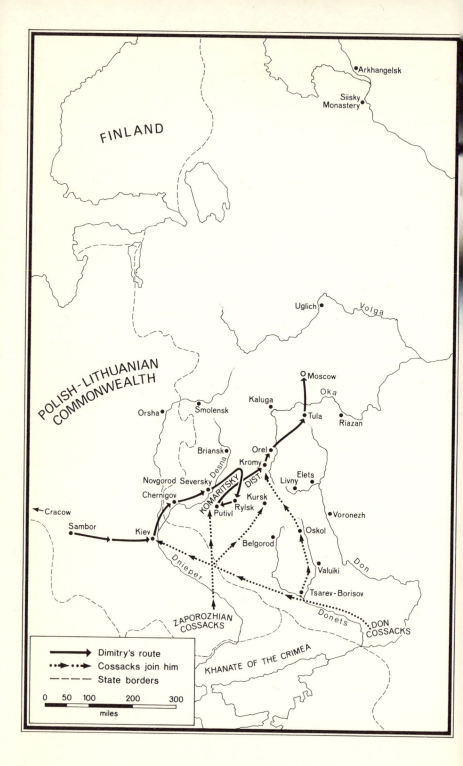

of the population of the Borderland, which here, too, easily fled state service for the Field, or if it served, it did so without any zeal. By the time of the appearance of the "true Tsarevich" in 1601-1603, circumstances had also created new causes for popular grumbling and excitation. Chief among these was an extraordinary famine, which had befallen the country as the result of a three-year crop failure. The horrors of the lean years were extreme, the proportions of the calamity staggering. The suffering of the people, which extended even to cannibalism, was made more severe by the shameless speculation in grain, involving not only market buyers but also very respectable people including abbots of monasteries and wealthy landowners.

No better was the administration which supervised the distribution of the tsar's alms and the sale of grain from the tsar's storehouses. It contrived to steal money and flour and to profit in every way at the expense of those who were starving nearby. If hunger, need, and unemployment drove many onto the highway for plunder and brigandage, the rapacity of the rich and the powerful, about which the dispatches of the government itself spoke without concealment, must have embittered the poor people against the powerful and lent simple banditry an aspect of social protest. Of just such a character were the activities of the brigand ataman Khlopko around Moscow itself. He not only pillaged "in isolated places," but many times opposed the tsar's voevodas until he was captured in a regular battle. Neither he nor his banditti let government forces take them alive: whoever survived from a battle ran off to the Borderland without offering submission. According to the calculation of one contemporary, in the first years of the seventeenth century more than 20,000 men capable of bearing arms had gone to the Borderland. Not all of them, of course, came from robber bands, but all were victims of the hard conditions of life created by the famine crisis.

During the time of famine many lords released their bondmen—household workers—to avoid feeding them, and these people found no refuge anywhere, since they had not received the mandatory releases from their lords. For them the Borderland was the single place where they could expect to rid themselves of dependence and need. Naturally the mood of these people was far from contented and tranquil. To the general conditions of the starving time were also joined political circumstances. In connection with rumors about the pretender and the plot of the Romanovs and Belsky, Boris had issued interdicts against certain boyars. These entailed, according to Muscovite custom, confiscation of boyar estates and liberation of their domestics with an admonition against anyone taking them in. And the very same Borderland and Field offered these people refuge, just as it had sheltered other oppressed and persecuted, hungry and homeless folk. On the Field these new arrivals constituted the most restive and exasperated element. Yet the population of the Muscovite South already serving the government in the new towns of the Field was also dissatisfied with its conditions of service. The impostor's "seductive letters" found fertile soil here. In sum, the people of the Borderland were ready to rise up against the center, enticed by the possibility of joining their vengeance on long-standing oppressors with aid to the oppressed "true Tsarevich." At the pretender's call, therefore, in the towns of the Field those servitors and free Cossacks for Dimitry—the military population of the fortified towns and the wandering inhabitants of Cossack plots, tents, and camps—fused together into a mass of "Cossacks"; and this whole mass moved northward to await union with "Tsar Dimitry" wherever he might indicate.

In this way the pretender's campaign against Boris immediately began on two fronts. In August, 1604, the pretender himself invaded the Muscovite State from Kiev and started up the course of the river Desna, along its right bank, hoping by this route to emerge at the upper reaches of the Oka, from where the commercial roads led to Moscow. At the same time the Cossack mass from the Field set out northward along the "Crimean roads," directing their march to rendezvous with the impostor somewhere near Orel or Kromy and from there to advance with him on Moscow via Kaluga or Tula. Meanwhile, the army of Boris was somewhat late with its own campaign against the pretender. As the assembly point for the main army Boris designated Briansk—a town situated equally close to Smolensk and to the Seversk border. No matter whence the foe might appear, from Orsha or from Kiev, the army at Briansk could rush to intercept him. When it became clear that the pretender was coming from the Seversk region, the voevodas proceeded there and arrived in time not at the border itself but at Novgorod Seversky, where they encountered the impostor. He had succeeded in taking the small towns along the Desna, even the town of Chernigov, but around Novgorod Seversky he was detained for a long time. The direct road northward to Moscow was firmly closed to him. But he received news that to the east of him, on the Field, town after town was recognizing his authority. In the course of two weeks Putivl, Rylsk, Sevsk, the Komaritsky district, Kursk, and Kromy all yielded to him. Then Belgorod and Tsarev-Borisov recognized him. The rapid submission of the Field and of the Borderland towns enticed the pretender onward. He gave up the siege of Novgorod Seversky and turned right, to the east toward Sevsk, for immediate junction with the Cossacks. However, Boris's voevodas overtook him en route and routed his handful of Polish-Lithuanian and Russian followers. The impostor then fled southward and, failing to unite with the Cossacks, shut himself up in stone-walled Putivl, having lost all his forces and with scant hope of personal salvation. It seemed his song had been sung.

The further insurrection of the Cossacks in the Muscovite Borderland saved him. Despite his defeat, the Cossacks continued to seize towns in his name. In Putivl the pretender learned that Oskol, Valuiki, Voronezh, Elets, and Livny had recognized him. The entire Field had been taken over by the movement against the Muscovite government, and the boyars at the head of Boris's army had to leave off pursuit of the pretender and lead their forces north in order to avoid being cut off from Moscow. The boyars retired toward the fortifications of Kromy, where there was an important junction of roads converging from the entire region seized by the revolt. Cossacks were already ensconced at Kromy. The Muscovite forces surrounded them and blocked their outlet northward to Moscow. This became the focus of military operations for a long time: the Cossacks were unable to move forward, while Boris's forces were unable to drive them out of Kromy southward. Thus passed the winter of 1604-1605. But in the early spring a decisive event occurred: Tsar Boris died on April 13, 1605.

4

Boris had been ailing since 1602, though he was far from old. What exactly he suffered from is difficult to establish. There is evidence that he was "hidropicus," that is, had dropsy from heart disease; in 1604 it was said that he had suffered a stroke, "dragged one leg behind," was frequently ill, and for long periods did not venture out. But all the same his death at fifty-three seemed so sudden and unexpected that some were prepared to attribute it to suicide. It was rumored that Boris had felt badly in the middle of the day, either during a reception of ambassadors or at the end of his dinner. There was barely enough time to give him the last rites and, according to the ancient custom, to tonsure him as a monk (with the name of Bogolep). That same day he departed to eternity.

Only three weeks after his death Boris's army near Kromy betrayed the Godunovs and went over to the "true Tsar Dimitry Ivanovich." After three more weeks Boris's family was taken from the palace to his old court, where on June 10 his widow and son were murdered and his daughter made a desecrated prisoner.

The tragedy of Boris ended with the destruction of his family and the complete "impoverishment" of all the Godunov kin, chiefly for the reason that this family, having turned itself into a dynasty, had been condemned to political isolation. More than once we have pointed out that the friendly ties which had bound together the court aristocracy under Tsar Feodor Ivanovich were broken by the quarrel of the Romanovs and Godunovs in 1598 during the contest for the tsar's throne. This quarrel gave birth to the possibility of the pretender intrigue, turning the name of Tsarevich Dimitry into an instrument of the struggle. Not without connection to this intrigue were the defeated Romanovs and their disintegrated alliance "of sworn friendship" with Boris. Boris and his kin alone remained to oppose the princely aristocracy, which he had humbled and weakened, but the latter were not reconciled and did not forget their past primacy. When the pretender appeared, this aristocracy, obedient to the personal authority and talent of Boris, served him. But when Boris died they declined to support his dynasty and to serve his family. Among this aristocracy all the old pretensions immediately revived, past resentments began to be talked over, and a feeling of vengeance and thirst for power developed. The princes knew perfectly well that the dynasty just founded by Boris possessed neither a representative sufficiently able and suitable to rule nor any influential party of adherents and admirers. It was weak, it would be easy to destroy, and it was in fact destroyed.

The young Tsar Feodor Borisovich recalled Prince Mstislavsky and the princes Shuisky from the army to Moscow, and in their place sent Prince Mikhail Petrovich Katyrev-Rostovsky and Peter Feodorovich Basmanov. The two princes Golitsyn, the brothers Vasily and Ivan Vasilievich, remained near Kromy. The changes of the voevodas in the Muscovite command were probably made from caution; yet they served to harm the Godunovs. The forces around Kromy proved to be under the influence of the princes Golitsyn, the most noble and prominent of all the voevodas, and of Peter Basmanov, who enjoyed popularity and military good fortune. Moreover,

Moscow naturally had to court Vasily Shuisky, whom it considered an eyewitness to the Uglich events of 1591 and a witness, if not of the death, then of the saving of young Dimitry.

The prince-boyars had made themselves masters of the situation both in the army and in the capital and quickly declared for "Tsar Dimitry Ivanovich" against the Godunovs. The Golitsyns and Basmanov brought the army over to the side of the pretender. And in Moscow itself Prince Vasily Shuisky not only did not counteract the overthrow of the Godunovs and the triumph of the pretender, but, according to some accounts, when questioned he testified secretly that the true tsarevich had been saved from murder; and subsequently, with a number of other boyars, he left Moscow for Tula to meet the new Tsar Dimitry. Thus the representatives of the princely aristocracy conducted themselves in the decisive moment of the Moscow drama. Their conduct dealt a mortal blow to the Godunovs, and it was said that Vasily Vasilievich Golitsyn did not even deny himself the satisfaction of being present during the final minutes of Boris's wife and son, Tsar Feodor Borisovich.

5

Apparently, further support of the pretender did not enter into the plans of the princes. Once having destroyed the Godunovs, they did not plan to allow the latter's antagonist to come to power, for they did not consider him the "true Tsarevich." Upon returning from Tula to Moscow, Vasily Shuisky launched some sort of agitation against Tsar Dimitry. But by that time the pretender's agents had already hastened to Moscow and the inhabitants of the city, convinced by Shuisky himself of the genuineness of the "Tsarevich," obeyed not the princes but the new government. The Shuiskys were arrested and exiled. In the meantime the pretender triumphantly entered Moscow on June 20, 1605, and a month later was crowned tsar in the Cathedral of the Assumption [Uspensky Sobor].

Several historians have had a tendency to picture the pretender as a man of remarkable mind and shrewdness. In his time those who served the impostor and who needed to justify their own intimacy and attachment to him created such a reputation for him. But to the bulk of the people and to the servitors in Moscow the new tsar immediately appeared in an unfavorable light. The very first days of his reign were darkened by the spectacle of a political execution: Vasily Shuisky was led out on the square and put to the block. The executioner had already lifted his ax when a pardon arrived and the punishment was reduced to banishment. Along with the pretender's supporters—the Cossack and Polish detachments that had accompanied him to Moscow—Polish-Lithuanian magnates had also arrived. All these people felt that the Muscovites were indebted to them for the good fortune of the dynasty's restoration, and that the new tsar owed his own success to them. The deportment of the newcomers was haughty and rude, their morals dissolute. They insulted and embittered the Muscovites, and the new tsar did not wish or was not able to quiet them. To be sure, he soon disbanded his soldiery; but in their place emigrants from Poland and Lithuania hurried to Moscow to seek court favors and profits, and the tsar was always surrounded by alien guests and a foreign guard. In their midst he did not conduct himself in a tsarish manner, not observing the zealous order or etiquette customary in Muscovy. Rumors circulated about his drinking bouts and debauchery; it was said that he hobnobbed with hostelers, broke horses, and wandered about Moscow in bad company; that he did not keep the fasts nor observe the old customs. By January, 1606, only half a year after Tsar Dimitry's arrival in Moscow, his secretary Jan Buczynski reported to him that according to rumor Moscow was completely convinced that Dimitry was not the real tsar. By this message Buczynski wanted to forewarn his master and make him more cautious.

If the Muscovite crowd had its own reasons for dissatisfaction with the tsar, the Muscovite aristocracy had special causes for discontent. Tsar Dimitry brought back to Moscow from exile and elevated the kin of his alleged "mother"—the Nagois. He restored the Romanovs and Belsky to their previous status. It seemed that in Moscow the group of the court aristocracy was being reconstituted, while representatives of the princely aristocracy were obviously pushed into the background. The Shuiskys, it is true, were returned from exile, but not restored to the tsar's favor; also excluded were the most prominent princes—the Golitsyns, the Kurakins, the Vorotynskys. The princely group, which had been about to take command of the political situation in Moscow, lost it once more. And not just this group but all the great boyars in general must have been indignant with Dimitry's new favorites, who took precedence at court. Among the latter Peter Basmanov seemed a very eminent man: the pretender's affection for him was shared by those "emaciated" princes like Masalsky and Tatev, such unpedigreed people as the state secretaries Afanasy Vlasiev and Bogdan Sutupov, and the noblemen Mikhalko Molchanov and Grigory Mikulin. These men were all upstarts. In company with the Lithuanians and the Poles they formed a ruling clique unacceptable to true Muscovites. Hardly had the Shuiskys returned to Moscow from exile than they contrived with the Golitsyns (at the beginning of 1606) to send a secret message to King Sigismund in Cracow. They complained that the king had sent them as tsar a base and frivolous person, who was cruel and given to dissipation and extravagance—in short, unfit to occupy the throne—therefore they hoped to overthrow him and requested Sigismund to give them his son Wladyslaw as tsar.

Thus, a few months were sufficient for the adventurer who had acceded to the throne of Muscovy to lose the confidence of and prestige in the most diverse circles of the capital, and he ceased to appear as the "true Tsarevich." Finally, he was ruined in the opinion of the Russian people when they became convinced of his non-Orthodoxy, "heresy," and predilection for unbelievers. The desire of the pretender to marry a Polish woman without her conversion to Orthodoxy, the admission of Catholics into Orthodox churches, the betrothal in absence of the fiancée according to the Catholic rite in Cracow —all this pushed the Orthodox clergy into the ranks of Tsar Dimitry's foes. Only a chief and leader was needed to rally the discontented and to organize an uprising. Such a head and leader proved to be the "first sufferer," whose head had once lain on the block—Prince Vasily Ivanovich Shuisky.

To prepare an uprising and to raise the mass of the populace in an organized movement, time was needed. Shuisky and his comrades used almost half a year for this. During this interval the pretender could have displayed his political capacities, if he had any, and could have reinforced his personal position. However, he succeeded only in revealing his own frivolousness. In relations with the Polish government he showed himself to be ungrateful and forgetful. He did not remember the aid that Sigismund had provided him; he did not want to fulfill the obligations assumed in Poland. In questions of etiquette and title he conducted himself arrogantly and pettily: when the Poles refused him the tsar's title and, as before, named the Muscovite tsar "grand prince," he demanded that they acknowledge him "emperor." By the time of his fall he had already forfeited all favor on the part of official Poland, just as he had succeeded in spoiling his relations with the Jesuits previously around him. The latter complained, though with restraint, that he shunned them, and that he not only evaded service to papal objectives but even avoided simple meetings with them. If we recall that with other countries besides Poland the pretender failed to develop any closeness or political friendship, then we shall understand that in the midst of a people discontented with him he was virtually alone. Several court favorites, the group of Polish guests and the *streltsy,* the palace guard whom the tsar showered with gifts— such was all the strength that Dimitry could muster to oppose an angry populace.

All this, of course, was taken into account by the Muscovite boyars. The princes, headed by Vasily Shuisky and several members of the Romanov circle who sided with him, decided to act immediately after the marriage of the impostor. The wedding with its excessive banqueting was celebrated in May, 1606, and served as the last drop which overflowed the cup of Muscovite patience. Along with the bride hundreds of Polish guests arrived for the ceremony. A festive people, they raised an uproar all over Moscow and behaved as if in a conquered city. Unbelievers were allowed in the Kremlin for the tsar's wedding, but the common Muscovite populace was not permitted in. The strict marriage rite was not observed; the very day of the wedding—May 8, on the eve of Friday and St. Nicholas's Day—was chosen against church regulation and custom. The feasting was too raucous and too protracted. In general the wedding stirred up and outraged all of Moscow. From May 12 onwards the populace as a whole began to be restive, aroused by the boyar conspirators. They brought people from their estates to Moscow and employed military detachments passing through the capital for service in southern towns.

The early morning of May 17 was fixed as the time to act. When the tocsin sounded at dawn, a mob rushed to slaughter and plunder the Poles and Lithuanians in the residences where they were staying; while amidst the tumult of the massacre some two hundred conspirators burst into the Kremlin, penetrated to the palace, and murdered Peter Basmanov and Tsar Dimitry himself. His wife Marina Mniszech and her relatives were seized and arrested. When the aim of the conspiracy had been achieved, its leaders began to quiet the populace and end the slaughter. In the streets appeared the princes Shuisky, Golitsyn, Mstislavsky, the boyars Ivan Nikitich Romanov, Feodor Ivanovich Sheremetiev, and the *okolnichy*[21] Mikhail Ignatievich Tatishchev. Everywhere they restored order, dispersed the mobs of ruffians, set up sentries for protection at

---

21. The second highest rank of the Muscovite service aristocracy after that of boyar. (T.)

Polish houses, and dispatched surviving foreigners to secure places. In short, they became a provisional government and obtained obedience. The *streltsy* forces obeyed them, and the administration functioned under their leadership.

In the massacre thousands of foreigners and adherents of the pretender perished. Moscow rid herself of all those she considered her enemies. May 17 and 18 were days of elemental ferment among the masses. But on May 19 a new tsar had already been chosen—Prince Vasily Ivanovich Shuisky—and, apparently, a new patriarch was also selected. When Dimitry had acceded to the throne and the Godunovs had fallen, their friend Patriarch Iov had fallen, too. Ignaty, the Greek metropolitan of Riazan, had replaced him. Now Ignaty had been brought low, and Feodor Romanov, the elder Filaret tonsured as a monk by order of Boris Godunov, was named Patriarch of All Russia. Just how the selection of the tsar and nomination of the patriarch were completed that day of May 19 is not exactly known. From this day onward, however, the political life of Moscow entered a new phase. The struggle for the throne was over; a period of protracted internecine strife now ensued.

The beginning of the period of open Troubles, as set forth by us, took place at the Muscovite court. There the struggle among the boyar families and circles had proceeded—at first for power and influence, later for the throne itself. The intrigues at court and the election struggle had sought to bring the mass of the populace into the political game. In Moscow itself the court factions had turned to the populace, raising the street mob either to riot or to petition (either Tsar Feodor or Boris). Later, in armed struggle Boris and the impostor had turned to the forces of the populace. Hatched in boyar circles at court, the pretender intrigue had aroused the entire Muscovite South against Moscow, skillfully exploiting class antagonism in the service of the dynastic struggle. But, having been drawn into politics, the mass of the people still played the passive role of a simple and scarcely conscious tool. They had secured victory for those in whom they believed and whom they blindly served, without so far putting forward demands of their own. But they were conscious of these demands and expressed them the minute they understood that their foes had exploited their efforts. The servitors and the Cossacks of the southern towns and Field had dispatched "Tsar Dimitry" to Moscow in hopes of receiving from him privileges and a lightening of their burdens. Yet hardly had they returned home from the campaign than they learned that their tsar in Moscow had been murdered, and that power had been seized by those very boyars from whom they had experienced only oppression and malice. A mood of puzzled surprise immediately crystallized among these people and took the form of acute hostility toward the boyar government in Moscow. The South rose up against the "wicked boyars" in an outburst of intense social hatred, and the Troubles took on a completely new character.

Chapter

THE
SECOND PERIOD
OF THE TROUBLES:
THE
SOCIAL STRUGGLE

I

The accession of Prince Vasily Ivanovich
Shuisky serves as the pretext for a popular
uprising.
1. The setting of Shuisky's accession.
2. The movement on the Field and in other
regions.
3. Bolotnikov and the "brigands" before Moscow, in Kaluga and in Tula; their defeat.

1

Tsar Vasily Ivanovich Shuisky was not "elected to the
throne" as Boris Godunov had been. No one mourned Tsar
Dimitry for forty days or summoned a "Sobor," but the deed
was accomplished in one day. On May 19 the conspirators—the
princes and boyars who had deposed the pretender—went to
the Kremlin, from where they took Prince Vasily to the *Lobnoe
Mesto* [22] on Red Square and there, amidst a crowd of the
populace, proclaimed him tsar. Then they accompanied him
to the Cathedral of the Assumption, where the new sovereign
immediately "kissed the cross to all the land," pledging that he
would not misuse the power given him. It was quite obvious
that the "election" was the work of the princely-boyar clique
which had seized power and in which Vasily Shuisky played
the leading role. This clique's brazen act prompted contemporaries to remark that even in Moscow, not to mention the rest
of the state, not everyone knew about Shuisky's election. As a
result the new tsar had to face the difficult problem of explain-
ing to his own subjects his unexpected accession and the sud-

---

22. That is, Place of the Skull, a sort of rostrum where proclamations were read and executions performed. (T.)

den overturn of May 17. Shuisky tried to accomplish this via his "circular dispatches," which were sent everywhere.

He explained to the people that Tsar Dimitry had proved to be the "unfrocked monk," "heretic," and impostor Grishka Otrepiev, who had schemed to exterminate Orthodoxy, to wipe out the boyars, and to give Russian lands to the Poles; therefore he had been deposed and killed. About himself Shuisky said that he had acceded to the "patrimony of his forefathers" by right of birth, as a representative of the older Rurikovich line—"according to the tsarish station of Our forefathers"—and at the same time "by supplication" of all the people of Muscovy. The popular (and moreover sham) election he relegated to second place, advancing his own hereditary right to the throne. As successor to the previous dynasty, he graciously informed the populace: "We wish to rule the Muscovite State just as Our forefathers, the great sovereigns, the Russian tsars, did, and you We wish to favor and to love more than previously." In support of this promise he "deigned" to kiss the cross as a pledge "to all the people of the Muscovite State that We shall judge them with true and just court and will not lay Our ban upon any man without cause or be unjust to any man because of his enemies." Translated into plain language, this meant that the tsar promised not to execute or to exile anyone without an investigation and a trial, not to hold responsible or to punish the innocent kin of those judged guilty, and not to listen to denunciations or informers.

In these promises is visible a formal limitation of the new autocrat's authority, which he voluntarily accepted to please the boyar-princes who had put him in power. Indeed, he was completely dependent upon his accomplices, with whom he had led the conspiracy and seized power. By eminence he was foremost among the prominent members of the princely clique and had therefore received the throne from them; yet he remained in their circle and was bound to it not only by a community of purely aristocratic convictions, but also by a certain compact, which was reflected in the "kissing of the cross." However, a diminution of the tsar's authority was not included among Shuisky's promises; the new tsar publicly announced that he intended "to hold the state" in the same manner as previous "great sovereigns." He only promised not to abuse the autocratic power, as his immediate predecessors—Ivan the Terrible and Boris Godunov—had done. They had exiled and punished without trial, had punished entire families for the guilt of one relative ("destroyed all kin," in the words of Prince Kurbsky[23]), and had developed the practice of denunciations to the level of a social calamity. Tsar Vasily renounced just such techniques as had been characteristic of the oprichnina epoch by making a pledge to all the people, promising them justice and legality but certainly not the abolition of autocracy. If we recall that Tsar Vasily did not in fact keep these promises, and that soon after his accession he "began to wreak vengeance on people displeasing to him," then we shall understand that his promise possessed no formal force, was not an obligation, and did not become an operative norm. It was simply an indication of the political course the government desired to follow in order to gain popular support.

Shuisky's original brief manifestoes were soon followed by new ones. In the very first weeks of his rule the tsar decided to transfer the body of the Uglich prince "Tsarevich Dimitry" to Moscow and to display it there to the people, thereby destroying any possibility of the pretender affair continuing or of a new false Dimitry appearing. A regular commission went to Uglich for this purpose. Simultaneously, in Moscow the new government searched through the pretender's papers and found there evidence of his allegedly reprehensible intimacy with and pliability toward Poland. By the time the tsarevich's body was brought to Moscow on June 2, 1606, a second circular dispatch had been drawn up, literately composed, in which the entire story of the pretender's overthrow was once more ex-

---

23. Boyar opponent of Ivan the Terrible who fled Muscovite service to the Polish Commonwealth, from where he carried on a famous polemic with the tsar. (T.)

pounded and his sins enumerated. Shuisky's accession was also recounted, as well as the transfer to Moscow of the remains of the real Tsarevich Dimitry and his canonization, since the undecayed relics supposedly healed believers from various maladies. Many copies of this circular dispatch were distributed throughout the state, and it should have decisively reassured Muscovites as to the legality of the overturn which had occurred in Moscow and the propriety of Tsar Vasily's accession.

But all the efforts of Shuisky and his supporters were in vain. The dispatches did not convince the people, nor did the relics of the tsarevich stop rumors that Tsar Dimitry had escaped from Shuisky and that he would soon reappear to reclaim the tsardom of Muscovy. The oligarchical government in Moscow itself failed to reconcile everyone and proved unable to control the state of the public mind. Out of caution Shuisky banished from the capital many of those who had served the pretender, and this naturally aroused dissatisfaction against him among their adherents. He failed to make peace with the Romanov group of families. At the moment of the *coup* several representatives of this group (Ivan Nikitich Romanov, Feodor Ivanovich Sheremetiev) had acted in concert with Shuisky and the princes. In recompense for such cooperation the group wished to see the patriarchate in the hands of Filaret Romanov, and in fact called him patriarch. But this seemed unacceptable to Shuisky. When the nominee for patriarch was sent off to Uglich after the body of the tsarevich, Tsar Vasily undertook to keep Filaret as Metropolitan of Rostov and earmarked the patriarchate for the Metropolitan of Kazan, Hermogen, whom he summoned to Moscow. Like the degraded Patriarch Filaret himself, the entire boyar circle supporting him painfully felt the insult; they neither forgot nor forgave Tsar Vasily and henceforth always stood in the camp of his foes. In sum, few among the capital's leading group of court and service aristocracy obediently and sympathetically recognized the government of Shuisky. That is why, from the beginning to the end of Shuiskys' revolt-plagued rule, there were so many plots and plotters against him.

Shuisky even failed to hold in submission his own electors—that Muscovite mob which unceasingly surged about on the Red Square in Kitai-gorod and on the Ivanovskaia Square in the Kremlin. Earlier this mob had been characterized by inertness, and it had even looked on calmly as Ivan the Terrible cut off the heads of hundreds, "and they flung the heads as far as the courtyard of Mstislavsky." After Ivan's death the mob had made attempts to intervene in court affairs, but under Boris the court had contrived to tame the square and to punish "muzhiks who were seditious." The Shuiskys were among the first Muscovite politicians to adopt the habit of calling upon the square. Under Boris they had incited "some trading muzhiks" to request Tsar Feodor, "for the sake of offspring," to divorce Tsarina Irina. After Boris's death Vasily Shuisky, by testifying to the genuineness of the impostor, had raised the mob against the Godunovs and thus destroyed them. Soon thereafter he had tried to rouse the very same mob against the pretender, for which he had nearly paid with his life. During the struggle of the pretender against Godunov the Muscovite crowd had already acquired a taste for politics, avidly seizing upon news and discussing it. Foreigners residing in Moscow at the time noted that the Muscovite rabble, aroused by political motives, had become receptive to suggestions of any kind and a threat to the social order in general. Having accomplished the *coup* of May 17 and the massacre of the Poles by the forces of that very mob, Tsar Vasily proved unable to quiet his ally or to restore it to its previous state of peace and obedience.

The square had discovered its own strength and become accustomed to action; confident that it would not be punished, the mob was agreeable (said a contemporary) to a weekly change of sovereigns in the hope of plunder. Though Shuisky maintained himself by this mob, he was unable to control it. The matter was even more complicated because his enemies were also calling clandestinely upon the Muscovite crowd, inciting it against the established tsar. Less than a week after his accession Shuisky had already been constrained to pacify an upheaval of the rabble, allegedly raised against him by Peter Sheremetiev. Subsequently an uninterrupted string of popular outbreaks ensued upon all sorts of pretexts. These lasted the entire reign of Tsar Vasily, until that day when the same mob which had installed Shuisky arranged a "rite" for him, that is, deposed him from the throne and took him back to his old boyar court.

2

So, neither the court nor the capital lent firm support to Tsar Vasily's authority; still, they tolerated it. Yet a good half of the regions of the Muscovite State openly refused to recognize the boyar tsar when they heard of his election. As soon as news of the Moscow *coup* reached the Borderland and the Field, Putivl immediately rebelled against Moscow, along with the other Seversk towns, Livny and Elets, followed by the entire Field as well. A little later the towns around Tula and in the Riazan area rose up. The movement spread even further, to the east of Riazan into the region of the Mordvinians, to the Tsna and Sura rivers. It crossed over the Volga to the Viatka and the Kama; distant Astrakhan also revolted. From another direction, confusion ensued in the western borderlands of the state—in the Tver, Pskov, and Novgorod localities. In places so widely separated from each other the movement was not, of course, uniform; it did not draw one and the same social stratum into the struggle, but pursued various aims.

To begin with, quite clear beneath all its complexity and of great significance was what occurred in the Muscovite South. Here it can be said that the movement of the years 1604-1605 was repeated to the letter: namely, all those towns that had joined the pretender during his campaign on Moscow rose up again for Tsar Dimitry. In Moscow it was also understood that Tsar Vasily now faced a revolt of that very Borderland which just a year before had been "profaned" and "darkened by the madness" of the affair of the impostor, and therefore Muscovites began to call the Borderland "the land of utter turmoil." One can explain in various ways the unanimous rebellion of the Borderland and Field population against Shuisky's government. Yet its fundamental cause is readily understandable. These people had linked their fate with the success of the pretender; hence his destruction threatened disaster to his supporters as well. The "boyars" had overthrown the pretender, a "boyar" tsar reigned in Moscow, and the aristocratic, even oligarchical character of boyar attitudes and motives was even clearer to contemporaries than to us. From Muscovite boyars the Borderland could only expect the kind of governmental activity that it could not endure. It had to prepare for political repression because of its service to the pretender and for a general tightening of the yoke of servitude. On the other hand, a "boyar" government made up of leading representatives of the upper landholding class could least of all count upon the sympathy and submission of the Borderland, which was overflowing with fugitives from boyar households and fields. Here social discord and animosity had to lead to open political antagonism. Rumors to the effect that Tsar Dimitry had been saved from Shuisky provided an excellent pretext for an immediate opening of hostilities.

The uprising in the Borderland expanded rapidly because it used the prepared pattern and old organization of the previous campaign. At that time general headquarters had been at Putivl, and military operations had focused upon Kromy. The aim of the movement had been the middle course of the Oka and the Moskva rivers. Exactly the same situation arose again in 1606. Putivl became the center of the movement, and the Putivl voevoda Prince Grigory Shakhovskoi was considered the chief of the insurgents. Servitors from the nearby towns and Cossack detachments from the Field—"all the rebels who also during the time of the Unfrocked One had gulped the blood of Christians"—turned in customary fashion to Putivl for orders and sent news and prisoners there. From Putivl, in the name of Tsar Dimitry (who was not there) and by the authority of Prince Shakhovskoi, the remarkable "great voevoda" Ivan Bolotnikov launched his operations. After collecting a force, he moved along the routes of the previous year through the Seversk localities to that same Kromy, where all the roads from the South to the upper reaches of the Oka converged. At Kromy he encountered Shuisky's voevoda, Prince Yury Trubetskoi, and forced him to retreat. With the departure of Trubetskoi the road to the middle Oka was opened to the insurgents, and Bolotnikov set off toward Moscow, drawing after him bands of servitors dissatisfied with the government from Tula, Kashira, Venev, Aleksin, and Riazan.

Advancing on Moscow in such a state, the insurgent force possessed no internal social unity. The "great voevoda" Ivan Bolotnikov had become renowned in the Borderland because he first set forth the aim of the insurrection as not only a political drive to overthrow Shuisky's boyar government, but also a social revolution to undo the system of bondage. Besides mounting a campaign on Moscow to restore Tsar Dimitry, who was not with him, Bolotnikov called for action against the ruling classes in general. The original texts of his proclamations have not come down to us, but Muscovite authorities refer to them. In terror they reported that appeals were coming from Bolotnikov's camp to Moscow and to the other towns for "all sorts of evil deeds, for murder and pillage." The rebels "order the slaves of boyars to slay their own masters, and promise them the masters' wives, patrimonies, and pomestie estates; and they bid the despicable and unspeakable brigands to slay the rich merchants and all trading folk and to plunder their chattels; and they summon the brigands to them and want to give them the rank of boyar, voevoda, *okolnichy*, and state secretary." To exterminate the representatives of authority, landownership, and industrial-commercial capital and to seize their goods— such was the program that Bolotnikov used to entice the mob from the Borderland. In Muscovite parlance this was open "brigandage," that is, crime, and so Bolotnikov's whole force received the name "brigands" [*vory*]. Approaching Moscow, they in fact carried out their leader's program. "The boyars' bondmen and peasants gathered," says a chronicler about Bolotnikov's movement, "and with them joined Borderland posad people, *streltsy*, and Cossacks, they began to seize voevodas in the cities and to place them in dungeons, to wreck the houses of their own boyars, to pillage their goods, to outrage their wives and children, and to take for themselves." Bolotnikov's force came up to Moscow with a definite bent, clearly intent on attempting an overthrow of the existing order from below. This was a great and unexpected innovation in the development of the Muscovite Troubles.

The movement against Shuisky took on a different coloration in the more northerly strip of towns along the Oka through which Bolotnikov's forces passed en route from Kromy to Moscow. In this area the corps of servitors was marked by extreme variety. In the lists of gentry and *deti boyarskie* and in the land registers, alongside princes driven to this border district by the oprichnina, appear all sorts of lesser folk recruited into state service from the neighboring Field and granted noble status. Here the upper strata of the service class were distinguished by arrogance and prosperity; whereas its lower segments, impoverished and poor in land, were ready to go to their own brothers as slaves or house servants, "to live at the church and be a sexton on the dais," or even to flee service for the free Cossacks. The native Riazan gentry in particular represented a wealthy group. In degree of landed prosperity and in service position they closely resembled the hereditary nobility of the capital, and they were marked by the same pride of caste and thirst for career as the latter. Nevertheless, the Riazanians were dissatisfied with the oligarchical government of the Muscovite boyars, because it manifestly gave hegemony to the principle of "pedigree" and thus closed the path to a broader career for people not of that "well-blooded" circle. In the heat of discontent the Riazanians were drawn into the insurgent movement and simultaneously with Bolotnikov the "whole town," about 400 gentry with their domestics, appeared before Moscow to restore Tsar Dimitry. Not for a minute, however, could they share the program of the "brigand" host, for they themselves were landowners and slaveholders, served as voevodas in the towns, and were, of course, personally interested in binding peasants and slaves to them. The "brigands" of Bolotnikov were their social foes, and joint operations by these two social groups were a patent anomaly.

3

In mid-October, 1606, the rebels approached Moscow and established camp in the nearby village of Kolomenskoe, threatening to storm the capital. Shuisky hastily collected reinforcements to strengthen the regular Moscow garrison. Inside Moscow, however, the defenders soon became convinced that there was no Tsar Dimitry in the camp of the insurgents, and that the desire for a social revolution reigned there. And the Riazanians who had arrived along with Bolotnikov also became convinced of this. After some hesitation the service gentry decided to break with their allies, the "brigands," and "on the fifteenth day of November, from them, from the evil heretics and pillagers and defilers, from Kolomenskoe they went to the sovereign Tsar and Grand Prince Vasily Ivanovich of All Russia with their guilt." This event, when the Riazanians "as a whole town went away from those brigands and came to Moscow," exerted decisive influence on the course of affairs. With the defection to his side of the Riazan gentry, Shuisky became stronger than the "brigands," so he counterattacked. The example of the Riazan gentry influenced the gentry detachments of other towns previously with Bolotnikov; in the decisive moment of battle they, too, betrayed him and went over to Tsar Vasily. The "brigands" were routed and driven from Kolomenskoe. With terrible severity Shuisky pursued them to Tula and Kaluga. All this took place in December, 1606.

The meaning of the events which had taken place was enormously important. As soon as the aspiration of the "brigand" mass for a drastic social overturn manifested itself independently of Tsar Dimitry's cause, the dynastic question took a back seat. Whether people believed in the existence of Dimitry or not made no difference; they no longer fought for him, but for a class interest. The bands which had arrived before Moscow to fight against the boyar government broke up into those social groups from which they had formed, forgetting what precisely had united them in one force. Social antagonism destroyed the political alliance, and a sifting out of social classes occurred. It became clear to everyone that although Shuisky's government was an oligarchy, it alone at the given moment could unite the conservative proprietary classes of the population. Therefore the bulk of the service gentry sided with Shuisky. For their part, the "brigands" seemingly forgot about the "true Tsar Dimitry" for whose sake they had begun their campaign.

Since it was considered important to have some kind of "Tsarevich" with them, various bands of free Cossacks began to invent pretenders in great numbers. In 1607 there appeared in Tula one "Tsarevich Peter Feodorovich" (supposedly the son of Tsar Feodor), who had come from the Terek across the Don and the Donets. Subsequently there appeared on the Field the tsareviches Avgust Prince Ivan, Lavrenty, Feodor, Klementy, Savely, Simeon, Vasily, Eroshka, Gavrilka, Martynka, and so forth. All of them were obliged to serve as the pretext for the operations of those bands which "escorted" them. Sometimes these activities were simple brigandage, sometimes they assumed an aspect of political action; but at their base always lay a feeling of class animosity toward the "wicked boyars," the oppressors of the deprived laboring mass. In effect, a pretender was looked upon as the generally accepted method of mounting a revolutionary outbreak.

In 1607 military operations definitely proceeded under the banner of a social struggle. Having driven the "brigands" away from Moscow, Shuisky saw that the matter was not yet finished. Civil war was in prospect. The "brigands" held the entire Muscovite South. Moreover, Bolotnikov was ensconced in Kaluga, "and with him were settled [there] more than ten thousands of various people with firearms." All these people were boyars' bondmen and Cossacks—irreconcilable foes of "boyar" authority. Shuisky besieged Kaluga in the winter of 1606-1607, but failed to take it. By the spring of 1607 it was said that more than 30,000 "brigands" had assembled in Tula. They rescued Bolotnikov from the siege, and he likewise moved to Tula. In this way Tula became the main camp of the "brigands," from where they were about to launch a new campaign on Moscow. But Shuisky did not permit them to. He assembled a large army and in June, 1607, after routing the "brigands" near Kashira, he approached Tula and besieged that fortress. The main forces of the "brigands" were surrounded there and held in check. Meanwhile Shuisky's light detachments hurried southward and there carried out a ruthless punitive expedition in the localities which had revolted. They laid waste, it can be said, the entire South. "By order of Tsar Vasily the Tatars and the Cheremis were to war against all the people of the Borderland and Seversk towns, to take them prisoner and to plunder their properties for their treason and their brigandage; for they have revolted, they have stood against the state, and they have killed the people of Tsar Vasily." In October, 1607, Shuisky succeeded in seizing Tula as well. There he captured all the leaders of the rebellion—the princes Grigory Shakhovskoi and Andrei Teliatevsky, Bolotnikov himself, "Tsarevich Peter Feodorovich," and others, besides about 20,000 men of the "brigand" army.

With the fall of Tula all hope vanished for the defeated "brigands" to carry out the overturn they had desired. Shuisky's victory was complete; it only remained for him to decide the fate of the captured "brigand" army and to achieve the pacification of the recalcitrant towns to the south. To Tsar Vasily it seemed the latter problem had almost been solved and the movement in the South suppressed. He therefore turned his attention to liquidating the "brigand" mob in Tula. Those principally guilty of rebellion and the most dangerous and irreconcilable of its participants were executed—"thrust in the water" or hanged. The rest Shuisky wished to return as peasants or slaves to their former lords, or to give them away to others. This was done in such a way that the gentry "took traitorous people out of prison in their own custody to Moscow, and to Serpukhov, and around Tula, and to other towns, and provided them with food and clothes; and having taken them from prison on custody, they held service indentures [*kabala*] on them in their name." Hence the "brigands" who had revolted against the system of bondage were once more enserfed. Subsequently a certain part of those captured—those comparatively less suspect—were taken by the government to the southern towns for service "in the old hearths." The remainder were set free. All these hungry and homeless people straggled off from the Tula localities to the southern Borderland, where they appeared, of course, as a most suitable contingent to spark new uprisings. One account contemporary to the Troubles says very expressively of these people that, having fled from Tula on their own, they constituted a force anew and once more raised a revolt bigger than the first, "and instead of quiet they raised a storm which is blowing up to the clouds and threatens multi-rebellious rains, not of water, but of blood." Here the account means a further onslaught of "brigands" against the state under the banners of a second false Dimitry.

The circumstances of the struggle with Bolotnikov matured in Shuisky the ultimate conviction that his opponents were led not by dynastic but by class motives, and that he, Shuisky, ought not limit himself to the struggle with the specter of a false Dimitry as he had done hitherto. Tsar Vasily understood that he faced a dangerous social foe, and that it was necessary to assemble all forces and means for his suppression, both by arms and by other measures. For the military campaign of 1607 Shuisky gathered a large army, extended the repression to the entire South, and mercilessly punished the "brigands" and returned them to servitude. Beyond that he also took legislative measures to contend with the revolutionary elements of society and to influence the social conditions which had given birth to and nourished the Troubles.

Beginning in the spring of 1607 Tsar Vasily issued a series of decrees aimed at regulating the relations of dependent people—serfs and slaves—to their lords and to the government. The general tendency of these measures was, so far as possible, to bind in place and subject to registration and governmental supervision the laboring group which had sought changes and which had caused the upheavals. All slaves were to be bound to their lords by a legal order. As one document put it, "do not hold a slave a single day without an indenture." All peasants on proprietary lands were to be bound to those who held them and to whom they were ascribed in the registry books; the right of peasant departure was in the future completely abrogated, and whoever accepted another's peasant was obliged to pay damages to his owner and a heavy fine "to the tsar-sovereign for accepting against the code." In addition, the district administration was itself obligated to search out and to return fugitive proprietary serfs without waiting for private suits about them [in court]; while the population of posads and rural districts was obligated to answer for the reception of runaways. All these arrangements attest that the government clearly understood the significance of the Troubles experienced, yet thought to deal with them via the route of simple repression, hoping for its lasting success. The victory over Bolotnikov in Tula decisively reinforced this hope. Shuisky celebrated the seizure of Tula as a complete triumph over the enemy and did not consider it necessary to make any kind of concessions to them. The system of bondage remained in previous force and received even clearer definition and immutability in law.

Thus ended the first act of the struggle of the enserfed mass against the state. Those who had rebelled against the old order had suffered defeat, while the boyar government had triumphed. In its person triumphed political reaction, led by the princes, and social conservatism, represented by the land-owning groups of the population which had supported the princes in the struggle against the "brigands."

II

The failure of the first uprising coincides with the beginning of a second, more complex one.
1. The second false Dimitry: the Lithuanians and Poles in his army.
2. His war with Tsar Vasily; Tushino and the blockade of Moscow.
3. The transfer of the struggle to the North; the victory of Tsar Vasily.

1

The second act of the Muscovite social struggle proved to be much more complex. Sweden and the Polish Common-wealth, the constant rivals of Muscovy, followed Muscovite affairs with great interest, considering all events from the stand-point of their own profit. Their attention was especially di-rected toward Muscovy because Charles IX of Sweden and Sigismund III of Poland were irreconcilable enemies and jeal-ous of each other in relation to Moscow. Polish success in Muscovy was looked upon as Swedish failure, and vice versa. Up to 1606 it was the Poles who had succeeded. They had participated in the triumph of the false Dimitry and, so it seemed from the outside, held sway in Moscow itself. Shuisky's *coup* of May, 1606, had destroyed this hegemony and had strained relations between Muscovy and the Polish Common-wealth. Naturally, Sweden immediately wished to exploit this situation for its own purposes. More than once, beginning in the summer of 1606, Charles IX proposed to aid Shuisky against his enemies. But Moscow was evasive because Shuisky saw no necessity for an alliance with the Swedes. Emboldened by his victories over the "brigands," he even ordered his voevodas to answer the Swedes with some haughtiness: "Our Great Sovereign needs no help from anyone; against all his foes he can stand without you and will not request aid from anyone, except God." The Swedes did not have to wait long for a complete change in Tsar Vasily's tone, but meanwhile they had to accept the Muscovite rejection and calmly await further events.

The attitude of the Polish-Lithuanian government and society was not so pacific. In the Moscow massacre of May 17-18, 1606, between 2,000 and 3,000 Lithuanians and Poles had perished. More than 500 men remained in Muscovite captivity, most of them from the staff of the Polish-Lithuanian embassy and the suite of "Tsarina" Marina. Diplomatic relations between Shuisky and Sigismund were therefore very unsettled. The Muscovite embassy dispatched to Lithuania after the overthrow of the pretender was badly received by the government and insulted by the populace. Passing through towns and gentry estates, the Muscovite envoys were vilified and cursed, bombarded with mud and stones, and threatened with death. Clearly, relations with Muscovy were hostile and threatened vengeance.

If the king did not demand immediate satisfaction from Moscow and take up arms against her, it was only because the Polish Commonwealth had its own troubles in the form of a "mutiny." The Muscovite emissaries distinctly depicted this revolt. "People have now become self-willed," they wrote. "There is dissension amidst their rebellion." Insurrection took hold of the entire country: "the knights and commoners of both lands (Poland and Lithuania) are at a meeting on the field of Sandomierz, but there has never been such a meeting; they cover 15 miles." According to the Muscovite envoys, the magnates at the gathering were divided into three categories: some "stand against the king," because they accuse him of many sins; others, in contrast, take his side; while a third group stands "apart" and watches "which side will be more right or stronger." Although the king emerged the victor from clashes with the magnates and defeated the "mutineers" when they ventured into open battle with him, the Polish-Lithuanian government was nevertheless paralyzed by the turmoil and had to confine itself to bitter altercations with Moscow. Yet the feeling of insult from the Moscow massacre did not die out in Polish-Lithuanian society and was set forth at the first convenient moment when both sides—the king and the opposition —tried to stoke and to fan the flames of Muscovite internecine strife so as to deal Muscovy all possible harm.

One must recall these circumstances when studying how a second false Dimitry appeared on the Muscovite-Lithuanian border, and how with him began the second act of the Muscovite social drama. The origin of this impostor is unknown, and historians have shown little interest in him. This is because the personality of the second false Dimitry was insignificant and his role passive. With all his frivolity, the first pretender had seemed to be a sincere and serious claimant; he had attracted his own supporters, subdued and inspired the masses, and been the actual leader (or one of the leaders) of the movement he had aroused. Moscow had good reason, however, to christen the second false Dimitry with the scornful sobriquet the "Brigand" [*Vor*], that is, a simple malefactor. He did not lead his adherents; they used him for their own purposes, as a convenient and submissive instrument for the achievement of criminal (by Muscovite lights) and destructive aims. Muscovites saw clearly that the Brigand peeked out from the arms of the Polish-Lithuanian leaders and their detachments around him, while Russian "brigands" played a secondary role under him. Muscovites therefore referred to the Brigand as an emissary from King Sigismund and tagged his army with the general name of "the Lithuanians" or "the Poles." Even in official acts —for example, in the text of the treaty of 1608 with Poland and Lithuania—the matter was represented as "that Brigand whom the king's people, Prince Roman Ruzhinskoi [Rozynski] and

Prince Adam Vishnevetskoi [Wisniowiecki] and their comrades, bring with them through the Muscovite State, calling him by the previous name the murdered Unfrocked One had taken— Tsarevich Dimitry Ivanovich."

In fact, the Brigand was thrust onto Muscovite soil from the Lithuanian border. He came to Starodub Seversky (or, more exactly, to Popova Gora) with a convoy from the Chechersk (Lithuanian) official Ragoza. Proclaiming himself in June, 1607, "Tsar Dimitry Ivanovich" saved from the Moscow massacre, the Brigand immediately turned to Lithuania for aid, and by the end of August military men from the Polish Commonwealth had joined him, led by commanders Mekhovetski and Budzil. These magnates assumed general leadership over all the Brigand's military forces, in the corps of which there were also "brigand" Cossacks from the Muscovite Borderland. Thus from the very beginning, primacy in the Brigand's operations fell to the Poles and Lithuanians, and he began to peer out from their arms.

In the course of a short time, indeed by the beginning of 1608, many Polish-Lithuanian "regiments" had thronged to the Brigand; for at that time, thanks to the "mutiny" in the Polish Commonwealth, there were many detachments prepared for a campaign, both those who had fought for the king against the mutineers, as well as the mutineers themselves. The latter escaped the king's repression by fleeing to Muscovy, hoping to obtain there security, booty, and glory. And their opponents, the supporters of the king, assembled forces with his permission and went there openly. The king was equally content with the departure of the former and the latter; it saved him the trouble and expenditures of liquidating the mutiny, while it damaged and weakened the neighboring Muscovite State to the profit of the Polish Commonwealth. Besides, all this satisfied the natural desire for revenge on perfidious Muscovy for the massacre perpetrated against the Poles and Lithuanians, and for the coercion of the Polish embassy held captive in Moscow. Impelled by just such motives, the magnate Jan Peter Sapieha, according to his biographer, collected 7,500 men for a campaign against Muscovy. His aim was to avenge the captivity and destruction in Moscow of the first pretender's Polish guests and to win glory for himself and his country by the exploits of his knights. For vengeance and glory Prince Roman Rozynski also joined the Brigand with a detachment of "nearly four thousand men." After these eminent leaders there followed less prominent ones: the Tyszkiewicz, Waleski, Wieloglowski, Rudnitski, Kruslinski, Zborowski, Mlotski, Wilamowski, and others. In such fashion a sizeable Polish-Lithuanian army formed around the Brigand, led from the spring of 1608 by Hetman [commander] Rozynski.

Russian—or, more precisely, Muscovite—detachments also joined this basic core of the Brigand's army. They could not, of course, compare in degree of military art with the regular Polish companies and formed an irregular force; but, gradually accumulating around the Brigand, they still made up a large contingent, with a definite battle order and favorite chiefs, atamen. In this force there were, first of all, "military servitors and common people" of those places in the Seversk Borderland where the Brigand had first shown himself and had received recognition. Then the Brigand was joined by those segments of Bolotnikov's army which had eluded the siege of Tula or had escaped prior to its capitulation; such were the bands of Ataman Ivan Zarutsky. Furthermore, haphazard bands of wandering Cossacks from the Don and the Dnieper joined the Brigand. Finally, at the very beginning of 1608 a Lithuanian expatriate, the exile "deprived of his honor" for mutiny, Aleksander Lisowski, commenced his own operation of gathering up fugitives from Tula. He went around the entire Muscovite Borderland, collecting along the roads the remnants of Bolotnikov's force that Shuisky had released to the south from captivity in Tula. From this muster he set up military contingents, supplying them with weapons and provisions from captured Borderland fortresses. As a result, "there were assembled with him thirty thousand Russians from the Borderland."

He revived, as it were, to new activity the force of Bolotnikov just shattered by Shuisky and brought it into the Brigand's service.

From the foregoing one can see what large means the Brigand came to wield, thanks to the support rendered him from the Polish Commonwealth. It was precisely from there that he got his initial strength and impetus; from there, too, he received aid in assembling and utilizing Muscovite opposition-ist elements dispersed earlier in the struggle. Due to external aid he grew into a fearsome foe for Shuisky. Yet it should be noted that he appeared on Muscovite soil perhaps later than his instigators had calculated. The Brigand had proclaimed himself in Starodub in the summer of 1607, when the siege of Tula was just beginning, and had been about to rush to its relief with his first forces. His task, obviously, was to fan the flames of Muscovite civil strife and to reinforce Bolotnikov and Tsarevich Peter. But he was too late: Tula capitulated before his arrival, and fearing to fall under the blows of the victors, he hastily withdrew. On Shuisky's side, it was a great mistake that upon taking Tula he did not continue his campaign to the south. This saved the Brigand and gave him an opportunity to get firmly established. Shuisky left Tula for Moscow and demobilized his army in the certainty that he had brought his repression to an end. But meanwhile, in the course of the winter of 1607-1608, the Brigand augmented his forces and worked out a plan of campaign for the next summer.

2

With the spring of 1608 a regular war began. The Brigand's Polish detachments advanced on Moscow from Orel via Bolkhov, Kaluga, and Mozhaisk, while from Smolensk Sapieha also came via Mozhaisk. Lisowski completed the move-ment to the east already described and via Zaraisk and Ko-lomna likewise turned toward Moscow. The fortunes of war were on the Brigand's side: the Muscovite forces yielded the road to him, and when it came to battle they suffered defeats.

Only the talented voevoda Prince Ivan Semenovich Kurakin succeeded in dealing a stinging blow to Lisowski between Kolomna and Moscow and seized his artillery, so that the latter's "brigands" appeared before Moscow somewhat late and in some disorder. However, the Brigand's other forces arrived at Moscow in a victorious march. The Brigand set up headquarters in the village of Tushino, in the valley cut by the ravines of the river Skhodnia, several miles from the walls of Moscow. This place proved to be inaccessible to Shuisky's troops; but it was not well suited for siege operations against Moscow because it was too distant from the city's fortifications. For observation of the enemy Shuisky established a "train," that is, a fortified camp, on the Khodynskoe Field between Moscow and Tushino, and there he placed part of the Moscow garrison. This train cut off the approaches to the city from the Tushinites and prevented them from launching a regular siege. In consequence, Hetman Rozynski resolved on a general engagement, hoping to storm Moscow in the event of victory. The battle took place on June 25, 1608, but yielded no results. Though they suffered great losses, the defenders repulsed the Tushinites from the city walls. Following this battle the Brigand sat passively in Tushino for two months.

It became clear that both the contending sides were sufficiently powerful and determined to make the struggle a protracted one. In the meantime both Moscow and Tushino received reinforcements. By the fall of 1608 the Tushinites decided to act. Since storming Moscow had failed, and siege had proved impossible, they tried to establish a blockade around the city. Instead of completely investing Moscow, they attempted to occupy and close all the most important roads around the city so as to interdict the delivery of supplies and arrival of reinforcements into the capital. The operation was carried out energetically. Sapieha and Lisowski took over all roads leading to the northern half of the state and went from Tushino to Suzdal and Vladimir, subjecting to Tushinite authority almost all of Zamoskovie up to the Volga and even crossing the river.

At the same time other Tushinite bands followed the course of the Oka to Kolomna. If they had seized Kolomna, from there they could have linked up with Vladimir and the ring of the blockade would have been closed. But Muscovite forces sent to the aid of the garrison repelled them from the town. Repeated attacks on Kolomna likewise failed because both Moscow and Riazan valued the connection enough to protect it from two sides. Via Kolomna, Moscow received grain from the Riazan region; whereas the Riazan gentry "upon the arrival of the brigands sent their wives and children to Moscow with their people," in order that "with the brigands' advance in the time of siege, being besieged, the wives and children should experience no privation." In this way a close bond was established between Moscow and Riazan. A break in contacts between the capital and this region provoked hunger in Moscow, and efforts immediately followed from both sides to restore the broken communications. Consequently, during the entire period of Moscow's struggle with Tushino not once did the Tushinites tightly close the Kolomna road. The ring of the blockade remained incomplete, and later, in 1609, it was also broken in other places.

The protracted character of the struggle obliged both sides to devise new and complex strategies. Shuisky decided to bring to the capital all the military forces he could collect from the most important fortresses. He ordered the borderland voevodas in Smolensk, Astrakhan, and Novgorod to set out with their garrisons toward Moscow and to collect en route all the fighting men that could be mobilized. To the northern towns he sent an exhortation to arm themselves, to send their levies to Yaroslavl, and to hold their own localities in order to prevent the Brigand from seizing the Pomorie. Simultaneously Shuisky began to contemplate foreign assistance. Having concluded a peace treaty in July, 1608, with Polish ambassadors in Moscow, he had included in it a provision that the king remove from the Muscovite State all the Polish-Lithuanian people serving the Brigand. This condition was very important to the

Muscovite diplomats. Although they did not count on much help from Sigismund, they thought that by recalling his subjects the king would materially weaken the Brigand (of course this did not happen, because the Tushinites did not obey the king). At the same time that he was settling with Sigismund, Shuisky was negotiating with the Swedes. He dispatched his relative Prince Mikhail Vasilievich Skopin-Shuisky to Novgorod with instructions to levy troops there, and in addition "to send to the 'Germans' to hire 'German' people for assistance." In such delicate form Muscovite statesmen clothed their turn to Sweden for alliance and auxiliary forces.

Such were the measures that Shuisky undertook, since he did not have strength enough to drive the Brigand away from Moscow. Meanwhile the Brigand, not having the strength to take Moscow, came to the conclusion that instead of a futile assault on the capital he ought to launch an offensive against the North; for with its conquest Moscow could not hold out. Still untouched by the Troubles, the North was then the richest region of the state, a gold mine from which it would be possible to draw great resources for the struggle, as well as choice spoils. Curtailing their operations around Moscow, the Tushinites turned across the Volga—principally to Vologda. In the town, according to their information, there were "many martens and sables and black foxes and all sorts of valuable wares and fine drink"; there were stored wares from the "English Germans" which had come via Arkhangelsk from across the sea; there gathered "all the best people, Muscovite merchants with great wares and with money, and the state treasury in Vologda is swollen from the ships' wharves, the sables from Siberia and foxes and all sorts of furs."

From their first foray the Tushinites succeeded in seizing many towns and districts in the North. They immediately instituted great levies "for Tsar Dimitry" in money and kind, which merged into outright plundering. But the matter was not limited to levies alone: Tushinite "magnates" installed themselves on private lands and in peasant districts, and they took billets on alien estates to feed both themselves and their retainers and horses. According to the local expression, the Tushinite authorities "in remuneration give away all the towns to the magnates as patrimonies." Such methods of administration aroused the local population, which saw in them a return to the hated past "when previously all had been appanages."

While the Tushinites were not in the North and were judged by hearsay, the northern towns and districts retained great coolness. From town to town they sent dispatches advising each other to pursue a cautious policy. They had already "given their souls" to Tsar Vasily at his accession and had no reason to hurry to change oaths and swear fidelity to a revitalized Tsar Dimitry. "Do not hasten to kiss the cross, one cannot guess what will happen," advised these simple-hearted opportunists. "It is still distant from us, we shall have time to submit." The North, in short, looked on attentively and bided its time. But when it realized the nature of the Tushinites, opportunism vanished. Comparing Shuisky's government with the Brigand's, the people of the North saw that the former preserved all the customary features of Muscovite rule, whereas the latter was foreign in personnel and "brigand" in method. The northern urban and rural communes were content with the Muscovite administration because its governing practice preserved the right of broad self-government to the local population. The Tushinite authorities, in contrast, scorned the peculiarities of local society and cruelly harassed and plundered the towns and rural districts they occupied. In response, the entire North revolted against the Brigand and the "magnates."

In customary fashion, just as was done at the tsar's command, northern "muzhiks" formed their own "companies," enlisting volunteers into them and supplying them with arms and all sorts of provisions. These companies were headed by elected leaders: those for whom "military affairs were a custom." A small-scale war was launched against the Tushinite bands operating in the North. Ustiuzhna, Kostroma, Galich,

Reshma, Yurievets-Povolzhsky, Gorodets, and Balakhna constituted the first line of resistance. Behind them Vologda, the most important town of the Pomorie, acted in a supporting capacity. In Vologda a council of defense was organized from Vologdians and from Muscovite merchants and government agents who were spending the winter there. Even foreign traders caught in the town by the Troubles were enlisted in the council. The Vologda council was in communication with the entire Pomorie, and via Ustiug it collected men and resources for the struggle, directing them to the southern positions. From the other side Skopin-Shuisky, who was then in Novgorod, established contact with Vologda and the other northern towns, sent them his own instructors ("chiefs"), and little by little assumed general leadership of the entire operation against the Tushinites.

At first the insurgents suffered heavy setbacks from the Polish cavalry of the Tushinites; but then they began to overpower the uncoordinated Tushinite detachments and to push them southward. In the spring of 1609 they had already completely driven the Tushinites from the left bank of the Volga and had thrown them back on their bases toward Dmitrov and Suzdal. The North was liberated from the "magnates" and the "brigands"; the "muzhiks," as they were scornfully called in Tushino, had prevailed. Crossing the Volga to the south, they prepared for a further struggle against the Brigand on behalf of Tsar Vasily.

The battle for the North had ended in Shuisky's favor. This was a very important victory. But it still remained to exploit this triumph, which Skopin-Shuisky did with great talent. In May, 1609, as soon as the Tushinites' failure along and across the Volga had become manifest, Skopin-Shuisky set out from Novgorod for Moscow with the forces he had collected. Under his command were about 3,000 Russian troops and some detachments of hired *Landsknechte,* which the king of Sweden had provided him in return for the cession of the Russian towns (from Yam to Korela) on the Finnish littoral. From

Novgorod, Skopin had already led the movement in the North for a long time. Now he demanded that the northern detachments join forces with him, and as an assembly point he named the Kaliazin Monastery on the Volga, hastening there himself. Then, in the fall, "joining with the Kostromites, and with the Yaroslavites, and with people from other towns," Skopin left Kaliazin, crossed the main road from Moscow to Yaroslavl, and fortified himself in Aleksandrova Sloboda. Here by his invitation the boyar Feodor Ivanovich Sheremetiev arrived from Nizhny Novgorod with the forces he had collected in the Lower Reaches (from Astrakhan to Nizhny).

Thus was achieved the union of Shuisky's fighting forces. A large army had been organized, supported by the northern regions of the state. The North had been decisively closed to the Brigand, and the Tushinites had been forced back to their old positions around Moscow itself. And in the winter of 1609-1610 Skopin launched a regular and cautious offensive against them. He advanced on Moscow by means of a running engagement, resorting to one and the same device on all the roads that he seized. He constructed fortified strongholds and placed garrisons in them which held the given route at their disposal. Slowly but surely he overpowered the enemy, and it was clear that all the strength was on his side. Under the threat of his blows the Brigand, after quarrelling with Rozynski, abandoned Tushino about January 1, 1610, and fled to Kaluga.

III

Muscovite civil strife provokes the intervention of King Sigismund.

1. The fall of Tushino and the treaty of the Tushinite nobility with the king in February, 1610.

2. The defeat of Tsar Vasily's forces at Klushino and his overthrow.

1

Tsar Vasily could celebrate a new triumph over his foes. Yet by now his fate was such that each moment of success was complicated by new misfortunes. His victory over the first pretender had brought Bolotnikov upon him; victory over Bolotnikov, the Brigand; over the Brigand, King Sigismund. Just as Skopin launched the campaign on Tushino from Aleksandrova Sloboda, the king opened military operations against Shuisky around Smolensk. The pretext for the king's hostile action was Shuisky's alliance with the Swedes, which put Muscovy in the ranks of Sigismund's foes. But the real cause of the campaign against Muscovy was, of course, the desire to exploit Muscovite internal dissension in the interests of Poland and of the king himself, and in addition to prevent Sweden from strengthening itself on Moscow's account. The king laid siege to Smolensk and sent envoys to Tushino to impress upon the Tushinite Poles that they should more properly serve him, the king, than the impostor. He demanded their adherence to the royal forces and promised them remuneration and rewards. When the king's emissaries appeared in Tushino, the Tushinites were already anticipating the approach of Skopin and their own imminent end. They greeted the Polish envoys with great irritation. The Cossacks and the "brigands" were not inclined to join with the Poles to serve the king. On their part, the king's emissaries treated the "brigands" and the impostor with utter scorn. Hence the Brigand did not consider it necessary to linger in Tushino and after a sharp quarrel with Rozynski went off to Kaluga, with the Cossacks flocking after him. Behind Kaluga's stone walls they hoped to sit out both Skopin and the Poles. The Poles who had served the Brigand were themselves little disposed to heed the king's call, but they understood that it was impossible to remain in Tushino. After long arguments they evacuated Tushino and went off toward Volokolamsk, and from Voloka they decided to disperse, each on his own. In March, 1610, Tushino was emptied; in it re-

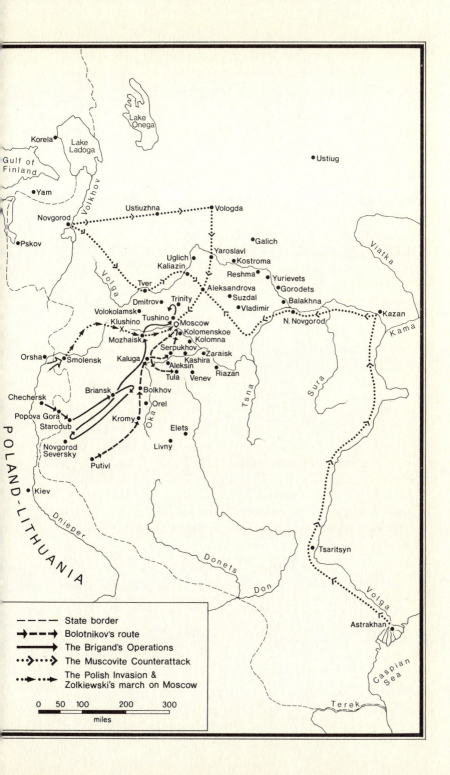

Korela
Lake Ladoga
Gulf of Finland
Yam
Novgorod
Pskov
Volkhov
Lake Onega
Ustiug
Ustiuzhna
Vologda
Galich
Volga
Uglich
Kaliazin
Yaroslavl
Kostroma
Tver
Reshma
Yurievets
Gorodets
Dmitrov
Trinity
Aleksandrova
Suzdal
Balakhna
Viatka
Volokolamsk
Klushino
Tushino
Moscow
Vladimir
N. Novgorod
Kazan
Kama
Mozhaisk
Kolomenskoe
Kolomna
Orsha
Smolensk
Kaluga
Serpukhov
Kashira
Zaraisk
Aleksin
Tula
Venev
Riazan
Tsna
Sura
Briansk
Bolkhov
Orel
Chechersk
Popova Gora
Starodub
Kromy
Oka
Elets
Livny
Novgorod
Seversky
Putivl
Kiev
Dnieper
POLAND-LITHUANIA
Donets
Don
Tsaritsyn
Volga
Astrakhan
Caspian Sea
Terek

State border
Bolotnikov's route
The Brigand's Operations
The Muscovite Counterattack
The Polish Invasion &
Zolkiewski's march on Moscow

0   50 100   200   300
miles

mained—and those not for long—only such Tushinites as did not belong either to the Polish contingents or to the corps of Cossacks. These were for the most part "migratory birds"— people who had come over to the Brigand from Moscow. Contemporaries wrote many curious things about them.

When the Brigand had settled down before Moscow in Tushino and nearly broken into the capital itself during the battle of June 25, 1608, the Muscovites had fallen into a panic and had imagined that the power of Shuisky was at an end. Purely from fear some decided to flee Moscow and to seek the Brigand's favor; yet others reckoned that an opportune moment had arrived to rise up against Tsar Vasily and thereby speed his fall. A contemporary notes that "after that battle (of June 25) there began to go off from Moscow to Tushino nobles of the table, [24] and nobles of the household, and Moscow gentry, and garrison gentry, and provincial gentry, and *deti boyarskie,* and clerks, and all sorts of people." At this time the princes Trubetskoi came to Tushino, and many people from families close to the Romanovs came: the Saltykovs, the princes Sitsky and Cherkassky, Ivan Ivanovich Godunov. Subsequently the princes Shakhovskoi appeared there, as did the Zasekins, the Boriatinskys, and many "good gentry" like the Buturlins, the Pleshcheevs, and others. After these migrants, strings of lesser people streamed out from Moscow. When the blockade dragged on, migrations became, one might say, an open practice.

Muscovites had come to a complete collapse of political discipline and morality. The court and service folk easily betrayed Tsar Vasily and went off to the "brigand encampments," but they returned just as easily to serve once more in Moscow, though ready on occasion to leave again for Tushino. This was possible because the two rivals—Shuisky and the Brigand—had the same need of men and valued them to an equal degree.

---

24. Rough English translations have been used for the various ranks of nobility mentioned here. For a listing of these ranks in their order of importance, see G. V. Lantzeff, *Siberia in the Seventeenth Century* (Berkeley, 1943), pp. 6-7, n. 23. (T.)

Cheap repentance for betrayal saved the "migratory birds" from punishment, and their impunity prompted others to imitate their example in order to receive "more honor and gifts and property than previously." Following the servitors simple folk flocked to Tushino. Solely for despicable profit Moscow hucksters brought goods by a roundabout path to Tushino; they "sold their own fathers and brothers for silver," as they even delivered to Tushino gunpowder from Moscow for the destruction of their fellow citizens. When calamity broke over Tushino, this whole crowd shrank back to Moscow or scattered about the nearby towns. In Tushino only those persons remained who had nowhere to run, who had firmly bound their fate and career to Tushino, or who were neither able nor willing to make peace with Tsar Vasily. Among them were the Tushinite nobility and the clever dealers who had run the Tushino administration.

First place among the Tushinite nobility belonged to Filaret Romanov. Under the first pretender he had been made Metropolitan of Rostov; upon Shuisky's accession he had at first been nominated Patriarch of All Russia, but a few days later had been demoted to his previous dignity of metropolitan and had been sent from Moscow to Rostov. At the establishment of Tushino in October, 1608, the Tushinites had taken him prisoner in Rostov and had taken him to the Brigand. The Brigand had acknowledged him Patriarch, and from that time onward Filaret had been in Tushino, according to some reports, as a captive, but according to others, as a free citizen and head of the clergy which recognized "Tsar Dimitry Ivanovich." There can be no doubt that Filaret did not believe in the authenticity of this tsar, but he did not want to serve Shuisky. He did not follow the Brigand when the latter fled from Tushino to Kaluga—but neither did he set out for Moscow, when he might have done so upon the breakup of Tushino.

Like Filaret himself, the Tushinite nobility grouped around him preferred to enter into contacts with King Sigismund. Following their example many of the non-noble people in Tushino were inclined to the same thing, attracted to the Brigand's service by private ambition or by accidental adversities and the danger of persecution and disgrace from Shuisky in Moscow. All this group "of the very poorest people, trading muzhiks, and young *deti boyarskie*" played a significant role at Tushino. The well-born servitors of the Brigand usually served as voevodas in the towns and armies, and only a few of them lived near the Brigand, whom they all shunned. Therefore, simple people, non-noble state secretaries, lesser *deti boyarskie*, and "muzhiks" headed the central organization of the Brigand. Not shrinking from the Brigand's situation, they constituted under him the circle that ran things. In view of the fall of their own "Tsar," they dared not return to Shuisky in Moscow, and they all straggled off after Filaret to the king.

When Sigismund's envoys to Tushino could not reach an agreement with the Poles there, they turned, at the king's instructions, to the Russian Tushinites, urging them to place themselves under his rule. According to the envoys' impression, the Russians accepted Sigismund's favor with the liveliest rejoicing. Yet they were reluctant to summon Sigismund himself to rule the Muscovite State, and instead requested him to grant his son Wladyslaw for the throne. In other words, Sigismund proposed the position of subjects to them, but they desired only a personal union. On this basis negotiations were begun between the king and the Russian Tushinites, and on February 4, 1610, a treaty was concluded in the king's camp before Smolensk. It was drawn up by senators named by the king and by emissaries from the Russian Tushinites: Mikhail Saltykov and his son Ivan, the princes Yury Dimitrievich Khvorostinin and Vasily Mikhailovich Mosalsky [Rubets-Masalsky], as well as gentry and state secretaries. The agreement of February 4 worked out the initial wording of a political treaty aimed at uniting the two hitherto hostile states. Although Muscovy was represented here by a chance company of Tushinite "migratory birds," the compact set forth clear and precise thoughts concerning the inviolability of the Muscovite religion and state order.

The treaty aimed to safeguard Muscovite life against any influence on the part of the Polish-Lithuanian government and society, obligating Wladyslaw to uphold without change Orthodoxy, the state order, and the estate order of Muscovy. The authority of Tsar Wladyslaw was to be limited by the Duma and the boyar judiciary, and by the council "of all the land," precisely with the aim of preserving and strengthening "all previous good customs" against possible infringements on the part of a central authority unaccustomed to Muscovite relationships. Thus a national-conservative character marked the agreement in general. But in it there were several details of a liberal nature. The treaty was very cool to the interests of the princely aristocracy which, headed by Tsar Vasily, was ruling at that very moment in Moscow; there is no mention of it in the text of the agreement. On the contrary, the treaty obligated the tsar "to raise the lesser dignity in consideration of its services," that is, to promote according to personal deserts persons of lower "dignity" (rank or calling). These peculiarities indicate, of course, that the group which made the agreement with Sigismund was itself not high-born and was at loggerheads with the princely-boyar Muscovite government.

When agreement with Sigismund had been reached and the Russian Tushinites had recognized Wladyslaw as their sovereign, they left Tushino for the king's camp in order to comprise there a directing staff for Muscovite affairs. Filaret was also about to set out after the others, but en route to Smolensk, in May, 1610, he was intercepted by Shuisky's forces and was taken to Moscow (with rejoicing at the liberation of this "captive" from hostile hands). With Filaret's arrival the idea of union with the Polish Commonwealth took root in Moscow. Originally expressed under the first pretender, when the Shuiskys and the Golitsyns had secretly requested Wladyslaw from Sigismund, this thought was now given clear and practical form. The king himself sent the February treaty to Moscow; but this royal communication could be hidden from the Muscovites by Shuisky. Filaret, however, had many means to circulate the news of the compact among his intimates and admirers. Later on we shall see that Filaret's appearance in Moscow greatly facilitated the overthrow of Shuisky.

2

Probably Tsar Vasily himself did not recognize in the spring of 1610 how shaky his position was. Spring began brightly and joyously for him. On March 6 the military men "with all the troops" evacuated Tushino with such haste that they left behind a huge supply of flour and grain, which was sent to Moscow. On March 12 the conqueror of the Brigand, Mikhail Skopin-Shuisky, arrived in Moscow. The capital revived, and "from all the towns to Moscow all sorts of people came with grain and with all kinds of victuals." Feasting and revelry began in the city. The political situation brightened. The Brigand had lost all significance and was sitting passively with the Cossacks in Kaluga. The Polish contingents that had served him dispersed—for the most part to join the king, but a minority transformed themselves into robber bands. In the interim Skopin concentrated his large military forces in Moscow. Included in their corps was the allied Swedish "armored detachment"—auxiliary forces composed of *Landsknechte*. This entire military mass could be hurled against the single remaining foe of Muscovy—Sigismund. After defeating him it would only remain to restore order in the exhausted country, and it seemed that the Troubles would then be over.

But this hope was not fated to be realized, and events menacing to Shuisky were once more about to darken the limpid stream of Muscovite life. In the second half of April, 1610, Prince Mikhail Vasilievich Skopin-Shuisky, the talented and popular youth in whom Muscovy saw a possible successor to the childless Tsar Vasily, fell ill and died in mysterious fashion. His sudden demise aroused rumors that his own kin, the Shuiskys, had poisoned him from envy of his glory. With Skopin's death Tsar Vasily lost the fidelity of the Riazan gentry, who believed the rumor about poisoning; in the dead leader he also lost the intermediary between his government and the northern "muzhiks" whom Skopin had armed and led to Moscow. The death of Skopin, as S. M. Soloviev has expressed it, "broke the tie of the Russian people with Shuisky" and deprived Tsar Vasily of moral support. Skopin's place in the impending campaign against Sigismund was assumed by Tsar Vasily's brother, Prince Dimitry Ivanovich Shuisky, an untalented and unpopular boyar. Of him a contemporary said that he was "at heart ferocious, yet not brave." He set out for Smolensk with the army against the king—"he left with a multitude of forces, but returned in terror," in the words of another contemporary. Taken by surprise en route by Hetman Zolkiewski, Shuisky had to accept battle where he had not anticipated it, and on June 24 at the village of Klushino (about 14 miles from Gzhatsk) he was defeated.

The consequences of this battle were terrible for Tsar Vasily. The Swedish forces formerly in the army of Dimitry Ivanovich Shuisky proved to be cut off from Moscow, and in part went over to the Poles, in part went off to the Swedish borders, to Novgorod Land. And the Muscovite troops, having dispersed after the battle to their towns and villages, did not further appear in Moscow, though the tsar sent after them. Meanwhile, the Riazanians—those same Riazanians who had sat out the entire siege of Moscow with Shuisky—flatly refused service to him; that is, they mutinied. Tsar Vasily no longer had any forces, while the victor, Hetman Zolkiewski, was approaching Moscow. Simultaneously, after learning of Tsar Vasily's misfortune, the Brigand also hastened from Kaluga toward Moscow. Hence Muscovites had to gird themselves for a renewed siege, to expect Zolkiewski by the Mozhaisk road and the Brigand by the Serpukhov and Kolomna roads. Their patience was exhausted, and Tsar Vasily's rule came to an end.

His had been a dreary reign. Tsar Vasily, "sitting in his own tsardom, suffered many misfortunes and disgrace and abuses," recalled a later chronicle. "Many sorrows and much anguish befell the sovereign," it was said of Shuisky in the seventeenth century. His self-willed seizure of power, arbitrariness and cruelty, despite solemn promises and the kissing of the cross, joined with Shuisky's personal weakness to deprive his government of the necessary moral force. "In his days every sort of justice fled, there was no true court, and every virtue was suppressed," one of the most intelligent writers of the seventeenth century, Prince Ivan Andreevich Khvorostinin, observed of Shuisky. Among the people it was said that Shuisky was unworthy of the throne: "Thanks to him much blood is spilled"; "he is an ill-fated sovereign"; "hunger and sword stem from the tsar's bad luck"; Tsar Vasily himself was "a stupid and dishonest person, a drunkard and a lecher."

Such views about Tsar Vasily, apparently general, led to frequent uprisings against him in Moscow. From the very first months of his reign the Muscovite mob was easily aroused against him, and in the difficult days of the Tushinite blockade this agitation attained great intensity. Worn out by high prices and hunger, the mob more than once raised the cry and rushed to the Kremlin. "*Deti boyarskie* and all sorts of 'black people' come to Shuisky with a cry and a wail and say: what do they have to wait for? Bread is dear, and there is no trade and nothing to take anywhere and nothing to buy it with!" Thus eyewitnesses describe the unrest then current in Moscow. And this turbulence frequently recurred, sometimes erupting into open revolts. For the time being Shuisky dealt with the malcontents, and after making some noise they escaped from the tsar to Tushino. Skopin's victory, of course, strengthened Shuisky, but the Klushino defeat, by infecting Muscovites with the threat of a new siege, destroyed him. Moscow took the tsardom away from him just as quickly and suddenly as he himself had earlier "vaulted" onto the throne.

The "rite" evidently happened to Shuisky as follows. The significance of the Klushino catastrophe was taken in by two cabals. In one the head was Prince Vasily Vasilievich Golitsyn, and the Riazan nobleman Prokopy Liapunov was its most zealous figure. Golitsyn wanted power for himself, but

Liapunov, his brothers, and other Riazanians were ready to work for him, and "they harbored a strong hostile aspiration against Tsar Vasily, in conspiracy with the boyar Prince Golitsyn." The other coterie of Shuisky's foes was headed by Filaret Romanov, while its main activists were those persons living in Moscow who were in touch with the group of Tushinites that had summoned Wladyslaw to the throne and who were receiving letters and "sheets" from the king in favor of his son. Most prominent among them were the Saltykovs, relatives of the Romanovs by marriage. They were solidly for Wladyslaw. Concealing their aspirations from each other, both conspiracies worked against the common enemy, and on July 17, 1610, when a popular movement broke out upon the Brigand of Kaluga's approach to Moscow, both exploited it. One of the Liapunovs, Zakhar, and Ivan Nikitich Saltykov led the crowd. The aroused mob proceeded from Red Square to a more open place—beyond the Arbat Gates to the Novodevichy Monastery. Several boyars and Patriarch Hermogen came there, and despite the admonitions of the patriarch, it was decided to ask Shuisky to surrender the throne and return to his old boyar court. Shuisky's brother-in-law, the boyar Prince Ivan Mikhailovich Vorotynsky, went to the Kremlin with other leaders of the mob, led Tsar Vasily out of the palace, and arrested his brothers. Then, so that Tsar Vasily could not return to the throne, he was forcibly tonsured as a monk and locked in the Kremlin's Chudov Monastery. Thus ended the four-year reign of the "boyar tsar," who had attempted to restore the political significance of the moribund princely aristocracy.

The overthrow of Tsar Vasily delivered the final blow to the Muscovite state order. The appearance of the Brigand had shattered state unity and had divided the country between two governments. Yet the fall of Tushino had been about to give hope of restoring this unity, when Shuisky's downfall destroyed all government. The country now had only pretenders to authority, but no real authority. The western regions of the state were occupied by the Swedes, who had seized

Novgorod after the battle of Klushino, and by the Poles, who were beleaguering Smolensk and had occupied Seversk Land. The Muscovite South was "in brigandage," that is, in complete anarchy; before the capital loomed the hostile armies of the Brigand and of Hetman Zolkiewski. The remaining parts of the state did not know whom to obey or whom to serve. In Moscow after Shuisky's overthrow the Boyar Duma assumed the role of a provisional government and wanted to summon delegates from the towns for the election of a tsar. But the towns barely obeyed this government and sent no delegates. Obviously the boyars had no real authority, either.

Such was the position of the Muscovite State in 1610. The second incursion of "brigands" into Muscovy, complicated by the participation of Lithuanians and Poles, had not given victory to the oppositionist mass. Nevertheless, it had shattered its foe—the oligarchical government of the princes—and had plunged the conservative strata of the population into anarchy and disorder. Both the contending sides were virtually beaten. Muscovite society, having lost political organization in the internal conflict, found no guiding forces within itself and fell victim to foreign conquerors, who opportunely and successfully intervened in Muscovite affairs for their own purposes. Such was the outcome of the Muscovite Troubles in their second period, which we have characterized as the period of the social struggle.

In the third period of the Troubles this social struggle of the lower and middle strata of Muscovite society continued, yet the primary fact of this period, which determined all the activities of Muscovites, was no longer civil strife but a struggle for nationhood against external enemies.

Chapter

THE
THIRD PERIOD
OF THE TROUBLES:
THE STRUGGLE
FOR NATIONHOOD

I

Moscow seeks escape from the Troubles in
dynastic union with the Polish Commonwealth.
1. The election of Prince Wladyslaw as tsar
and the embassy to Sigismund.
2. The policy of the king; the occupation of
Moscow by the Poles and the emergence of
Patriarch Hermogen against them.

1

The popular gathering that deposed Shuisky gave provisional power to the Boyar Duma, which at that moment
acted in a body of seven boyars—the prince Feodor Ivanovich
Mstislavsky "and comrades" (hence the name *semiboyar-
shchina* ["seven-boyar rule"]). Moscow swore fidelity to the
boyars, asking them "to stand up for the Muscovite State and
to judge us all after a fair trial and to elect a sovereign for the
Muscovite State with us, with all sorts of people from all the
land, in accordance with the [provincial] towns." Soon after
June 17 the boyars sent out invitations to the towns to send
delegates, "one man from each rank." But in those turbulent
days the invitations were not sent very punctually, and the
country did not respond to them. The boyars officially admitted after a month that "from the towns so far no people
have come" to Moscow.

Meanwhile events followed their own course. While the
Muscovites were considering whom to choose for the throne—a
Muscovite man of their own or a foreigner—Hetman Zolkiewski
neared Moscow with a Polish army. With him he brought the
candidacy of Wladyslaw, chosen by the Tushinite boyars a half-
year previously. This election was well known in Moscow, and
Wladyslaw had many partisans there, especially among the

upper aristocracy. While the clergy and the Muscovite mob discussed electing a tsar from the Golitsyn or the Romanov families, the boyars preferred Wladyslaw; for from Shuisky's example they had seen the total fiasco of an experiment with a tsar chosen from among themselves. The approach of Zolkiewski demanded rapid resolution of the matter. The proposal to convene a Zemsky Sobor with delegates from the towns fell through. The "seven-fold boyars" decided to convene a Zemsky Sobor by the old system, from those social elements that were in Moscow at that moment. To this Sobor they proposed the election of Wladyslaw upon conditions drawn up independently of the Tushino treaty of February 4. The Sobor obediently followed the boyars, and they received the opportunity to open negotiations with Zolkiewski in the name of "all the land" and "all ranks." They promptly concluded an agreement with the hetman and brought Moscow to swear fidelity to Tsar Wladyslaw. When in this manner the hetman had been converted from an enemy into an ally, the boyars turned him against the Brigand, whose Cossacks had advanced on Moscow but were now driven back to Kaluga. Then the boyars admitted the hetman and his forces into the inner forts of Moscow —in other words, gave up the capital to him. They acted thus from fear of the people of the capital. In the troubled days of the governmental overturn, voices in the Moscow mob had spoken in favor of the Brigand, and his "sheets" (proclamations) had been circulated about the city. The boyars feared "brigand" opposition so much that they resorted to the hetman for aid to protect the interests of Wladyslaw, whom they had elected.

The conditions proposed by the boyars to Wladyslaw and accepted by Zolkiewski repeated in substance the principles placed at the head of the treaty of February 4: inviolability of religion and the state order, political independence and separate status for the Muscovite State. But if the treaty of February 4, marked as it had been by a national-conservative character, had still envisaged several innovations, the Moscow treaty of

August 17 was notable for its irreconcilable conservatism. It was drawn up in a spirit of strict governmental traditions, with the firm intention to protect and to guarantee the bases of the Muscovite ecclesiastical, state, and social order against any encroachments not only by Polish-Lithuanian authorities but by native Muscovite innovators as well. In the August treaty there had vanished the articles about raising persons of lesser "station" in accordance with their personal service, about the freedom of departure abroad, and so on. Here, in contrast, there appeared a demand for the protection of the "patronymic"[25] and "honor" of Muscovite princely and boyar families, and the limits of the elected sovereign's authority were precisely indicated anew: He was obliged to accept Orthodoxy and to rule in conjunction with the Boyar Duma and the Zemsky Sobor. The highest court and the imposition of new taxes were reserved to the Boyar Duma; for legislation "all the land" was to be summoned. Obviously, this version of the treaty came from strictly conservative boyar circles, which aimed to strengthen the age-old Muscovite social order and to indicate to all Muscovite "stations" their proper—from the boyar point of view—place. This is why the treaty wholly deserves the label of "boyar."

Having disposed of this matter with the hetman, the boyars equipped a "grand embassy" to visit King Sigismund at Smolensk. It was to request the king to grant them Wladyslaw as tsar and to send him soon to Moscow. From its composition the embassy really was "grand" (that is, important, extraordinary). It comprised Filaret Romanov from the clergy and Prince Vasily Golitsyn from the Boyar Duma—both with the title of "grand envoy"; they were accompanied by members of the Zemsky Sobor. From the Sobor—"from all the land," as Golitsyn phrased it at Smolensk—were sent, first, every man of the less numerous estate groups (the provincial gentry) and, second, elected representatives of the more numerous groups (the capital gentry). In this way a significant part of the Sobor

---

25. That is, the old-established hierarchical order of the aristocratic families. (T.)

went to the king. The other part of it remained in Moscow. The Muscovite government was thereby divided, and the part that left on the embassy, without those who stayed behind in Moscow, was just as incompetent as the Moscow part was without those sent off to the king. This circumstance proved very important in the subsequent course of the king's relations with Muscovy.

<h1 style="text-align:center">2</h1>

Evidently not all the participants in the affair of Wladyslaw's election comprehended the complexity and intricacy of the political situation. More perspicacious and shrewd than all was Hetman Zolkiewski. In the negotiations with the boyars he appeared gentle and pliable. He promised that Wladyslaw would accept the Muscovite faith; he nobly helped Moscow to rid herself of the Brigand; he won the confidence of the boyars and of the patriarch and succeeded in occupying the capital. Moscow saw a friend in him. At the same time he influenced the selection of the grand emissaries in such a way as to achieve the removal from Moscow of Wladyslaw's rival, Prince Golitsyn, and the head of the Romanov family, Filaret, whose son Mikhail some intended for tsar. Both these dangerous rivals of Sigismund turned up in his hands when they came as envoys to his camp before Smolensk. The hetman even contrived to spirit away to the king the former tsar Vasily Shuisky[26] and his brother Dimitry. In short, Zolkiewski did everything he could to master the Muscovite State. Yet he understood that such brilliant success had been achieved accidentally, by a propitious confluence of circumstances; that Muscovy had neither been subdued nor captured, but had voluntarily entered into the agreement; and that one had to be wary and cautious in dealing with her. He reported to the king in this sense.

Sigismund, however, saw things differently: to him it seemed that the Muscovite State lay shattered at his feet, con-

---

26. Vasily Shuisky (1552-1612) subsequently died in Poland. (T.)

quered by his sword. Hence he had no need to enter into an agreement with the defeated enemy or to sacrifice the faith of his own son, but he would command Muscovy and bluntly subordinate her to royal authority. Sigismund reprimanded the hetman for his supposed weakness and received the grand embassy with the veiled intention of forcing it to accept himself instead of Wladyslaw for the throne.

As soon as the king's short-sighted and stubborn policy became clear to Zolkiewski, he took leave and departed for home, turning over command in Moscow to Aleksander Gosiewski. Without Zolkiewski the king ran things in his own way and without constraints. By his wish Gosiewski set up in Moscow a Polish military dictatorship in whose grip the boyars, in their own words, "at that time were not all alive." They were deprived of all significance because Gosiewski, "without considering Muscovite custom, transferred to himself all affairs." To assist him, Sigismund sent to Moscow members of the Tushino clique who had fled from there to him and who, having summoned Wladyslaw as tsar, had obediently begun to serve Sigismund himself. According to Muscovite conceptions, these were "the very worst people": minor scribes, "little *deti boyarskie*," even "trading muzhiks." (Among them, especially noticeable were Feodor Andronov, a "muzhik," and Ivan Gramotin, a clerk.) All of this crowd, whom Moscow greeted with distrust and derision, were indiscriminately accepted into Gosiewski's service. In consequence, after the Time of Troubles the boyars, meeting Gosiewski and recalling his actions in Moscow, told him to his face: "To the boyars (in the Duma) thou didst come bringing petitions; only, having come, thou didst sit down, and around thee didst seat thy councillors, Mikhail Saltykov, Prince Vasily Mosalsky, Fedka Andronov, Ivan Gramotin, and their comrades, but it was not for us to hear what thou with thy councillors didst speak and discuss; and what thou badest be done on any petition, thus they did, and they signed [i.e., resolved] petitions, thy own councillors, the state secretaries Ivan Gramotin, Evdokim Vitovtov, Ivan Chicherin, and from the trading muzhiks Stepanka Solovetskoi; whereas the old state secretaries thou didst drive all away."

The humiliation of the boyars went so far that without the slightest foundation Gosiewski ordered their arrest and openly took the government of Moscow into his own hands, debarring the boyars from all affairs and subordinating them to his own caprice. The boyars "put their signatures as they were ordered"; they were "just the same as in captivity"; "they only sat and watched." Thus Sigismund implemented his rule in Moscow.

For the embassy before Smolensk things were no better than for the boyars in Moscow. Only a little time and wit were necessary to realize that the king would not give his son for the Muscovite throne but intended to seize it for himself. For the time being the king's diplomats still negotiated with the grand emissaries about the agreement reached in Moscow. From this it became clear that the embassy could only negotiate within the limits of its "instruction" and had no right to concede anything from the conditions worked out with the hetman in Moscow; while in the absence of the grand embassy the part of the Zemsky Sobor remaining in Moscow was equally incompetent to change anything in the agreement previously accepted. Then, having sized up the state of affairs, Sigismund made an attempt to return the Muscovite embassy to Moscow so that there "all the land" might elect him as tsar instead of Wladyslaw. The grand emissaries themselves did not go to Moscow; but other members of the embassy—and quite a few of them— were enticed to return, the king bringing them around to his own point of view "by fear and by flattery." The embassy fell apart. Thus, though the king failed to force the Muscovite government voluntarily and publicly to recognize himself instead of Wladyslaw as tsar of "all Russia," in practice he did succeed in destroying that government and seizing power in Moscow. When he had finally achieved this, he arrested the grand ambassadors and dispatched them to Poland. Accordingly, at the end of 1610 the Muscovite State had no authority of its own; in it reigned a foreign dictatorship.

The attempt at political union with the Polish Commonwealth was the swan song of the Muscovite boyar class. Having received supreme power in their own hands after the overturn of May, 1606, the boyar-princes had made an attempt "to rule the Russian Land by [their own] general council," electing one of themselves to the throne. This attempt had proved abortive; the country had denied its sympathy to the oligarchs, and within the boyar group itself there had been no unanimity. The boyar tsar did not survive the Troubles. Then the ruling class turned to the idea of union, of attracting to the Muscovite throne a neutral figure from outside. If this course had succeeded, the "seven-fold" boyars who had invited Wladyslaw would have become the mainstays of a ruling class, participating in power upon the basis of an exactly defined right. But the affair miscarried. Polish force oppressed and humiliated the boyars. Furthermore, by linking the Boyar Duma with the names of Wladyslaw and Sigismund, the Polish dictatorship cast a shadow of "treason" over the boyars. It seemed that they must be working for the alien power if they did not suffer from it. The populace accordingly regarded some boyars as martyrs, others as traitors, and understood that the Boyar Duma had ceased to be a guide for the country. In the words of a contemporary, "wise elders became scarce and the good councillors became powerless." Sigismund delivered the final blow to the boyars, forever destroying their political significance and that of the Duma. In place of the class shattered in the struggle other social forces had to emerge.

It is easy to imagine the confusion with which the Russian people observed the first signs of Sigismund's cupidity. Wladyslaw did not come to Moscow; the grand emissaries wrote secret letters with warnings about the king's plans; former Tushinites appeared in Moscow with royal mandates and instructions. All this bewildered and disturbed the Muscovites. The more impressionable among them (the princes Vorotynsky and Andrei Vasilievich Golitsyn) had already become so alarmed in October, 1610, that they were arrested by Gosiewski. By November all Moscow was astir, but the Polish authorities took extraordinary measures to put the city on a military footing. Sentries were placed on the walls of the capital; patrols were sent about the streets; the populace was forbidden to carry arms; the protective trellises blocking the streets were broken up; the neighboring peasantry was not permitted into the city; nocturnal movement was stopped. By December the people of Moscow already knew that all was not well with Wladyslaw, and that Sigismund himself wanted to be tsar. In the Cathedral of the Assumption, Patriarch Hermogen began to speak about this to the people. He flatly forbade his flock to kiss the cross to the Catholic king.

This opposition of the patriarch had an extremely important significance. First, it revealed the urgency of the crisis to the bulk of the people and, second, it brought Hermogen into the political arena. Heretofore Hermogen's political role had not been great. There was nothing of the political activist in him. Unreceptive and obstinate (according to the old expression, "stagnant"), not far-sighted ("about good and evil not rapidly enlightened," and a "believer in rumor"), Hermogen commanded neither flexibility of mind nor breadth of vision. He was not always able to orient himself well in a complex situation, and under Shuisky he had more than once been deceived and enthralled by the cunning tsar, with whom he was on bad terms, or by the mass movement of the mob, which he did not know how to control. Still, he had not agreed to the election of Wladyslaw either quickly or easily, but having fallen under Zolkiewski's personal charm, he had nonetheless gone along with the boyar government. Yet when the fiasco of this government became manifest and the pretensions of Sigismund were revealed, Hermogen displayed his basic qualities. He was not frightened by Gosiewski or by the king's other agents. He felt himself to be the head of the church and was conscious of his duty to the faithful. He found the courage to impress upon the populace that while preserving their oath of fidelity to Wladyslaw, if he accepted conversion to Orthodoxy, they should in no way swear allegiance to Sigismund himself. Warning his flock against the king, Hermogen also came into open opposition to Gosiewski, to the frightened boyars, and to the king's agents who headed the Muscovite government. A contest ensued between the church hierarchy and the supporters of the king—a struggle which gave Hermogen the glory of a "second *Zlatoust*"[27] and placed him at the head of a national movement against the Poles. Contemporaries highly valued the patriarch's patriotic initiative: "If the patriarch had not been sent by God and undertaken such a miraculous affair, who would have taken his place? If even the Poles had wanted to trample the faith and put topknots on everyone [i.e., to Polonize them], nobody would dare say a word!"

In brief, Hermogen alone opened the eyes of the Russian people and by his perseverance saved the Muscovite State from ultimate enslavement. Such was his significance at this point in the flow of events.

---

27. *Zlatoust*—"golden-tongued"—referred to St. John Chrysostom (347-407), archbishop of Constantinople and celebrated orator. (T.)

II

King Sigismund's policy provokes a popular uprising against him.
1. The formation of a popular militia and its variegated composition.
2. The siege of Moscow and the popular government.
3. The "compact" of June 30, 1611; the collapse of the militia as a result of internal dissension; the triumph of the Cossacks.

1

The patriarch's open emergence against the king, which occurred about December 1, 1610, coincided with the unexpected death of the Brigand, murdered by his own followers in Kaluga on December 11. If the voice of the patriarch indicated the necessity of resistance to the king, the death of the Brigand untied hands for operations against the Poles without the apprehension of a blow from the rear. Therefore, in the middle of December an abrupt shift took place in the mood of Moscow. Active propaganda commenced for a rising against the Poles, and it was conducted in the name of the patriarch, although Hermogen himself had evidently not yet called for "boldness and bloodshed against the foes." From Moscow the idea of an uprising spread throughout the country. Everywhere a moral crisis ripened—in the camp of the Muscovite emissaries before the walls of beleaguered Smolensk; in the Moscow administrative departments subordinate to Tushinite petty folk who had become the king's agents; on the streets of Moscow under the surveillance of the Polish sentry; and finally, in the towns and villages under the oppression of Polish military requisitioning and billeting—everywhere the general danger stilled private passions and desires and called forth higher gusts of popular feeling.

The country was preparing for a struggle and searching for leaders. It unanimously considered the patriarch its spiritual leader, while military leaders appeared by themselves. Of course, primary significance in the popular movement must have been assumed by the most prominent figures of provincial society: namely, the voevodas and gentry of the leading towns and districts, the elected authorities of the more populous and prosperous communes, as well as the atamen and leaders by other names of those detachments—Cossack, Lithuanian, Polish —which had survived from the Tushinite organization and which were opposed to the king.

About January 1, 1611, the Poles, by their own account,

intercepted several dispatches from Hermogen to the towns with a summons that "everyone, having gathered together in an assemblage from all the towns, shall come to Moscow against the Lithuanian people." Such dispatches have not come down to us, but there can scarcely be any doubt that in launching the "assemblage" the townspeople were in communication with the patriarch and anticipated his approval, or that the patriarch did not refuse them his blessing.

In spiritual agreement with the church hierarchy, one of the first towns to rebel was Riazan with its voevoda, Prokopy Petrovich Liapunov. Simultaneously with Riazan rose Nizhny Novgorod, which had maintained secret contacts with Hermogen through special messengers who fearlessly penetrated to the patriarch even when Gosiewski placed him under arrest. Following Riazan and Nizhny many other towns revolted. All the remnants of the Tushinite Cossacks and "brigand" forces also joined the movement. With special zeal Liapunov established contact with these social elements; for him, peace and alliance with the "brigand" army were a necessity from purely military considerations. Out of these contacts it emerged that among the former Tushinites the most prominent leaders against the Poles were ataman Ivan Zarutsky in Tula and the boyar Prince Dimitry Trubetskoi in Kaluga. Liapunov succeeded in reaching agreement with both of them, and the new allies worked out a "compact of all the land: to assemble in two towns, Kolomna and Serpukhov." In Kolomna the urban detachments from Riazan, the lower Oka, and the Kliazma were to gather, while in Serpukhov a special army of the old Tushinite detachments from Kaluga, Tula, and the Seversk region was to assemble. The "compact" was executed, and by March, 1611, the movement of military forces had begun. Popular and Cossack armies simultaneously hurried toward Moscow.

Naturally the Polish garrison occupying Moscow knew about the movement set in motion against it and took its own measures. Its strength did not suffice to defend the entire outer line of Moscow fortresses (the "Earthen Town [*Zemlianoi gorod*], along the line of the present Sadovaia Street), as well as the stone wall of the White Town [*Belyi gorod*] (along the line of the present boulevards). The Poles could successfully occupy only the interior Moscow citadels—the Kremlin and the Walled Town [*Kitai-gorod*]. They brought them onto a siege footing and, following the custom of the time, they decided to burn the rest of the city at the approach of the besiegers in order to deprive them of cover close to the fortress walls.

The Muscovites themselves helped the Poles arrange this matter by triggering a riot and street fight with them. On March 19 the fighting developed into a general battle. The Poles drove the Muscovite populace out of the Walled Town into the White Town and set the latter afire. Moscow burned down, and thousands of Muscovites were scattered about the environs without food or shelter. Advance detachments of the popular militia failed to arrive in time for this battle and found only the smoldering ruins of the capital. They established a camp, "encampments," on the ruins of Moscow. Following the advance guard the entire popular army arrived at Moscow and, having fortified itself in the encampments, undertook to besiege the Kremlin and the Walled Town. Thus began the summer of 1611.

In the new situation, with the entire country aroused against Wladyslaw and Sigismund, the Boyar Duma in Moscow lost all significance and ceased to be a government. The boyars were looked upon as traitors locked up in the siege with the foreign foe, toward whom they remained submissive. In place of this previous government it was necessary to create a new one. It could consist of those elements of authority which had appeared during the popular movement. Such figures as the Riazan voevoda Liapunov, the Tushino (later Kaluga) boyar Prince Dimitry Trubetskoi, the Cossack atamen Zarutsky and Prosovetsky already wielded authority over their own forces and over those districts and towns which they had occupied. Before Moscow they enlisted the services of their own local chanceries *(prikazy)* and through them continued to administer the bases from which they had collected forces, launched the campaign, and drawn the means for their support. But all these separate and uncoordinated *prikazy* did not constitute a regular apparatus of government. The need of one was sharply felt; it was indispensable to create a government. And one was created by uniting the various councils grouped around the most eminent leaders.

Taken together they called themselves "all the land" and descriptively named themselves "the boyars and voevodas, and the Duma gentleman Prokopy Petrovich Liapunov, and the *deti boyarskie* of all the towns, and all sorts of service people." From "all the land" they gave orders to the towns and districts, and the "compact" of all the land was considered the law of the country. Compacts of this sort had already been in force since April, 1611. According to all indications, however, the first attempts of "all the land" were not successful. Internal frictions existed in the popular militia, and at their base still lay the same social dissension between the Cossacks and the comparatively higher social strata—the landowning gentry and the well-to-do commercial-industrial posad population.

It has been noted above that in launching the movement in Riazan, Liapunov had been in communication with remnants of the "brigand" Tushinite army, which after the Brigand's death had lost all concentration or bond and were holed up in the southern half of the state, unable to determine their own future operations. They willingly joined the popular movement against Sigismund, and Liapunov promptly entered into alliance with them, hoping to channel the ferment of this dangerous mass into a more constructive direction in the struggle for the common popular cause "against the destroyers of the Christian Faith." Perhaps this was not completely circumspect. Once Liapunov had become closely associated with "brigand councillors" and the Cossacks, he had to accept all the consequences of this rapprochement and consider all the "brigands" and Cossacks fighters worthy of reward for their

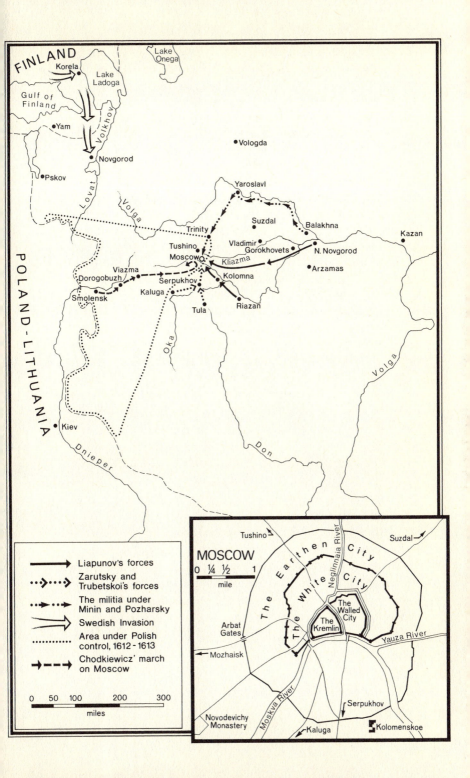

FINLAND

Korela
Lake Ladoga
Gulf of Finland
Lake Onega
Yam
Novgorod
Pskov
Vologda
Volkhov
Lovat
Volga
Yaroslavl
Suzdal
Balakhna
Kazan
Trinity
Tushino
Vladimir
Gorokhovets
N. Novgorod
POLAND - LITHUANIA
Moscow
Kliazma
Viazma
Dorogobuzh
Serpukhov
Arzamas
Smolensk
Kaluga
Kolomna
Tula
Riazan
Oka
Kiev
Dnieper
Don
Volga

MOSCOW

0   ¼   ½   1
        mile

Tushino
Suzdal
The Earthen City
Neglinnaia River
The White City
The Walled City
The Kremlin
Arbat Gates
Yauza River
Mozhaisk
Serpukhov
Moskva River
Novodevichy Monastery
Kaluga
Kolomenskoe

Liapunov's forces
Zarutsky and Trubetskoi's forces
The militia under Minin and Pozharsky
Swedish Invasion
Area under Polish control, 1612 - 1613
Chodkiewicz' march on Moscow

0   50   100   200   300
                miles

patriotic exploit. Liapunov imagined that the best reward for the dependent "boyar people," who at that time made up the "brigand" Cossack power, would be "freedom and remuneration." So he wrote with the promise of these to all Cossacks in general, inviting them to come and help him before Moscow. As regards fugitive slaves who had not yet become Cossacks, he added: "And let those boyar people, whether bondmen by deed or by ancestry, come without any doubt or fears; they will all have freedom and remuneration like other Cossacks."

One can surmise that this summons aimed to attract to Moscow all the wandering Cossacks on the Field, to direct their forces for the common cause, and by putting them on the payroll of the popular militia, to render the restless Cossack mass harmless to the social order. But if such were Liapunov's plans and hopes, he was cruelly mistaken. His call facilitated the gathering of large masses of Cossacks in the center of the state. Before Moscow a multitude of boyar serfs and free Cossacks assembled, expecting freedom and demanding remuneration but remaining in previous "brigandage" and not one bit reconciled to the old Muscovite order. In the militia of 1611 before Moscow, just exactly as in Bolotnikov's movement of 1606, irreconcilable social antagonists appeared in political alliance against a common foe. Their animosity made itself felt in the general council of the entire army. "Brigand" radicalism provoked a conservative reaction, and matters manifestly moved toward rupture and collapse of the militia. In June, 1611, the danger of internal collapse forced Liapunov to resort to an extreme measure. At his initiative the council of the entire army —"all the land," as it was called—resolved to provide the country with a new supreme government and to solve the most urgent problems of the current social scene by one solemn act. In the last days of June "all the land" worked out and on June 30 confirmed a "compact" that created a provisional government in the country, with defined powers and tasks in the sphere of social-class and agrarian policy.

3

The "compact of June 30" considered the supreme authority in the state to be "all the land," as personified in the council of the army, that is, the representatives of the constituent parts of the army before Moscow. "All the land" elected "into the government" boyars and voevodas (Trubetskoi, Liapunov, and Zarutsky). But this "government" was only a subordinate power, limited in its actions by the military council of "all the land." It was "not to inflict capital punishment on anyone without consulting 'all the land,' and not to banish to the towns; and whosoever shall kill anyone without the compact of the land shall himself be punished with death." The "government" received exactly defined compensation for its labor; whereas those lands which "the boyars have seized for themselves without the compact of the land and those they have given away" to others were liable to be returned to the state land fund. For the government's guidance, indications of the normal land provision from this fund were established for the entire army before Moscow in general and for other members of the servitor class in particular. Then followed a definition of Cossack remuneration: "old" Cossacks who had long served in detachments from the towns or in bands from the Field had the choice of receiving a pomestie estate and becoming servitor-pomeshchiks or, if they remained Cossacks, of receiving a bread ration and money for their service.

The "compact" next indicated the order of administration for the whole state. Instead of the many *prikazy* which existed in the various regiments, it set up general institutions for the entire country—appointments and pomestie estate *prikazy* for military personnel and affairs, financial *prikazy* for the collection and disbursement of money, *prikazy* for criminal affairs and police. Finally, the compact reaffirmed the old Muscovite rule by which the peasant's right of departure was considered abrogated: transported and fugitive "peasants and bondmen shall be given back to their old masters." This was an indirect but sharp thrust at those Cossack elements which did not fall under the conception of "old Cossacks," who had served "of old." Earlier Liapunov had enticed these elements with the promise of freedom and reward; now upon the investigation of their previous lords they were to be returned into bondage. A no less sharp enactment against the Cossacks—old and recent alike—consisted in not appointing them and their atamen to posts in the local administration of the towns and districts, and more generally in not allowing them out of the encampments before Moscow except under the leadership of "good gentry."

The whole content of the "compact" of June 30 attests that it was directed against the Cossacks and was intended to secure victory for the old Muscovite serf order. Obviously Liapunov, the representative of that order, at the given moment felt himself and his side to be stronger than the Cossacks and their leaders, the Tushinite boyar Trubetskoi and Ataman Zarutsky, and so he "ordered that the compact be written" to his own taste. However, this triumph of Liapunov was fragile and short-lived. The compact antagonized the Cossack side of the army before Moscow. At this moment, too, the principle of serfdom served as the main cause of sharp social conflict between the landholding gentry class of the army and its lower classes, which represented the organized oppositionist mass of the population. The Cossacks lured Liapunov into their "circle" for some sort of explanation and murdered him on July 22, 1611, then pillaged his "house" in the camp before Moscow and declared open war on the gentry. Having lost their unity with Liapunov's demise, the service gentry were forced to flee. "Many scattered from the Tsar's city," note contemporaries, and little by little "all departed from Moscow." The militia had collapsed. In it only Cossacks remained, along with those gentry "who were in brigandage at Tushino and at Kaluga."

In other words, the Tushinite camp was reborn before Moscow. But in Moscow itself there no longer existed a Russian authority that might have constituted a counterweight to "brigandage"; in Moscow there was only "treason" and Polish domination. Therefore the "brigand" Cossack authorities appeared as the central government for the entire country. They controlled the central governmental mechanism; with them in the encampments "in the appointments and in the pomestie estate *prikazy* and in the other *prikazy* sat state secretaries and clerks; and from the towns and rural districts they collected provisions for the Cossacks and brought them to Moscow." Having achieved power, the Cossacks "did not abandon their previous brigandage; they rode along the roads in bands and plundered." In such brief phrases contemporaries depicted "the real misfortune of the Muscovite State."

Undertaken by the Muscovite boyars, the first attempt to end the Troubles and to restore the state order through union with the Polish Commonwealth had led to a Polish military dictatorship. The second attempt, undertaken by the middle strata of the population with the help of the Cossacks, had led to the collapse of the popular militia and to the triumph of the Cossacks over the gentry. Having won power before Moscow, the Cossack encampment became the governing center of the entire country and at first, it seemed, had gained victory over the old Muscovite social order. Insufficiently cautious about allying with the "brigands," Muscovites of the middle class had hoped to discipline them, yet had themselves failed to withstand the Cossacks and had yielded the field of action to them. If there had been definite social ideals and creative inclinations among the Cossacks of that time, these might have become manifest in the activity of the Cossack government before Moscow. But there was none. The Cossack authorities only "collected provisions," while the Cossack bands rode along the roads and pillaged. The country could not subordinate itself to such a government.

III

The fiasco of the first uprising calls forth its more successful repetition.
1. The role of the clergy in 1611: the "dispatch" of Hermogen.
2. The movement in Nizhny Novgorod; its leaders; its program.
3. The formation of a provisional government ("all the land") in Yaroslavl and its policy.
4. Its victory over the Cossacks and the Poles; the liberation of Moscow.

1

The catastrophe before Moscow was not the only misfortune of the given moment. The flight of the service gentry from before Moscow and the transformation of the popular government into a Cossack-dominated one coincided with Sigismund's seizure of Smolensk and his imprisonment of the "grand ambassadors" Filaret and Golitsyn, and with the Swedish occupation of Novgorod and its region; while in Moscow itself the Poles imprisoned the patriarch and oppressed the boyars. All this shocked the minds and troubled the souls of the Muscovites; all this hinted at the possibility of complete destruction. The autumn of 1611 was a cheerless time for Muscovite society, tortured by an awareness of its own powerlessness. The Russian people had lost all hope and only prayed that the Lord would spare "a remnant of Christendom" and protect with peace "a remnant of the Russian realms and towns and countryside." From a once glorious state only "remnants" survived; no books "have ever spoken of such a punishment to any monarchy, tsardom or principality, as has been visited upon most exalted Russia."

The main misfortune, of course, was that the population did not know whom to obey nor whom to support. Both authorities—the Poles in Moscow and the Cossacks before Moscow—were unacceptable; the former were hostile and traitorous, the latter "brigandlike." Having lost its customary organization and center, the country now had no leaders or rulers who, like Skopin and Liapunov, might have drawn the bulk of the people into a popular movement, providing direction and a program through their leadership. Passionately desiring salvation and rebirth, Muscovites sought them in miracles and visions and turned to prayer and fasting in the hope of saving themselves by moral cleansing and renewal. Accounts circulated of miraculous phenomena and signs at the basis of which lay precisely a summons to repent. One such account even prompted an official decree from the Cossack encampments to fast for three days; and indeed fasting increased throughout the land and was so zealous that "many babies died from that fast." Other people, more even-tempered and resolute, tried to find an escape from the abyss, offering this or that practical counsel, presenting this or that program of action. There were many such proposals and programs, but they all boiled down to two basic and original ones.

One program was hastily and briefly expounded in Patriarch Hermogen's "dispatch" to the inhabitants of Nizhny Novgorod in the middle of August, 1611. The other consisted of the remarkable dispatches from the brotherhood of the Holy Trinity Monastery. It is a very curious circumstance that the initiative in a matter of political counsel and leadership issued from spiritual figures. This meant that the church had not collapsed along with the state, and that its representatives comprehended that they now had the duty to stand at the head of society, which had been deranged by the Troubles. But amidst the general ruin the voices of the church also resounded unequally and spoke differently; the writings of the patriarch and of the Trinity monks did not agree and were therefore incompatible. One had to choose between them.

The patriarch, held under guard in the Kremlin, learned that in the Cossacks' camp before Moscow Ataman Zarutsky desired "for the throne the son of the accursed Polish noblewoman Marinka," begotten in Tushino of Marina Mniszech by the Brigand. This outgrowth of the pretender affair greatly disturbed Hermogen. At the first opportunity, through a trusted and fearless man, Rodia Moseev, he secretly informed the inhabitants of Nizhny Novgorod, with whom he was in contact, that they should make every effort to spread this disquieting news about the towns and, in the name of the patriach, forbid recognition of the "Baby Brigand" [*Vorenok*] as tsar. Thus Hermogen requested them to carry his "word" against the Cossacks everywhere, to the towns and to the regiments, and "to say fearlessly that the accursed Baby Brigand is by no means acceptable." All those who revered the patriarch and desired to follow him must have concluded at the given moment that he considered the country's primary foe to be the Cossacks with their Baby Brigand, and that the primary task was to struggle against the impostor and the Cossacks. Indeed, in this letter Hermogen did not even mention the Poles or the king.

The dispatches sent from the Holy Trinity–St. Sergius Monastery were of a different content and tendency. In the Tushinite period the Trinity Monastery had withstood a long siege by Sapieha and Lisowski. Saved by its stone walls, the monastery had nevertheless been completely exhausted and ravaged by the deprivations of the siege. To restore the cloister after the siege Archimandrite Dionisy, one of the most remarkable persons of that time, was named father superior of the monastery. He took a broad approach to the task at hand. From the rich estates of the monastery preserved from destruction, and from other monasteries subordinate to Trinity Monastery, he drew the people and means to set his own monastery on its feet. Yet he did not begin to calm the brotherhood with "broad living," but on the contrary directed them toward labors for the common good. Situated some forty miles from

Moscow, the monastery was a witness to the "boiling" confusion: "by all paths fugitives came" to the Trinity cloister, inside the walls of which one could hide and rest and receive nourishment. Dionisy directed the efforts of his brotherhood to the organization of relief. The monks and monastery servants and peasants built hospitals, "houses and huts of various sorts for the reception of all sorts of rank." They collected supplies for the maintenance of the needs in these hospitals and houses; they nursed and fed the sick and the weak. They buried the dead. "Along the roads and forests they went and saw to it that wild beasts did not eat the deceased, and those tortured by the foes, the dead and the dying, they collected all."

Activity of this sort extended far beyond the walls of the cloister and needed the defense and patronage of authority. Yet at that time the single power upon which the monastery might lean was the militia before Moscow, at first the militia "of the land" under Liapunov, and later the Cossacks. By the force of things Dionisy came into contact with the "encampments," accepted aid and defense from Zarutsky and Trubetskoi, and in return helped them as much as he could in the struggle against the Poles. He sent "Trinity servants and servitors on foot with lead and potion (gunpowder)" and wrote "dispatches to all the towns about aid." These dispatches attained wide currency. They were addressed to the people of the countryside as a whole and summoned them to aid the Cossack army before Moscow against the Poles and the traitors who were with them in the capital. The monks did not shut their eyes to Cossack "brigandage"; nevertheless, they believed in the possibility of joint action and in a strong unity of the Cossacks with the middle classes of the population, whose differences they depicted as temporary and accidental. Therefore, during the entire second half of 1611 they preached unity with the Cossacks and in this respect differed radically from the patriarch. The latter issued the slogan: first against the Cossacks, then against the Poles. The monks, however, summoned all to join in concert with the Cossacks against the Poles. These were incompatible slogans, and the country, as we shall see further, followed not the Trinity brotherhood but Hermogen.

2

The collapse of Liapunov's militia had taken place in August, 1611, and by the end of that month the entire country already knew about the misfortune which had transpired. Hermogen's brief dispatch concerning the Baby Brigand reached Nizhny Novgorod on August 25, and immediately Nizhny and its neighboring towns communicated among themselves and agreed "to be one in counsel and in union," not to accept the Cossack government, and not to allow the Cossacks into town. Hermogen's urgent request was thus put into execution. The towns of the middle Volga declared themselves against the Cossack encampments, while the latter in their turn began to look upon the towns of the Lower Reaches as refractory rebels against the "boyars" before Moscow, Trubetskoi and Zarutsky.

Several weeks passed, and in Nizhny a further step was taken—from passive resistance to the Cossacks to active counter-measures against them. About September 1 one Kuzma Minin, a trader "who feeds himself from the poor business of selling," was elected into the group of communal elders who ran the communal economy and fiscal affairs of the Nizhny Novgorod posad. Entering upon his duties in September, he began to speak "before all in the communal office and elsewhere," discussing the necessity of an "undertaking" against the enemy, that is, instead of passively waiting to proceed to action. Great inspiration distinguished Minin's exhortation; by all accounts he was a man of great temperament and exceptional abilities. He succeeded in persuading his fellow citizens, and they did what they could according to their circumstances.

In the communal office, where all communal affairs were transacted, the posad people drew up a "compact of all the town under hands" (that is, with signatures, formal and firm). It proclaimed a special levy "for an organization of military men," and commissioned Minin to carry out this levy. First conceived by the posad, the matter was then submitted to the voevodas of Nizhny Novgorod, Prince Vasily Andreevich Zvenigorodsky and Andrei Semenovich Aliabiev. They revealed it to the whole town at a general town meeting of Nizhnyites of all classes. It was arranged, according to tradition, very solemnly: "before the holy gates" in the cathedral the archpriest Savva Efimiev read a dispatch from the Trinity Monastery and made a speech to the populace. After him spoke Minin. It was decided by the entire town to collect funds and to organize an army "for the cleansing of the Muscovite State." Minin became the elected communal commissioner for the money levy, the "tax assessor," in the customary expression of that time. Power over the militia, which was to be organized with public funds, was delegated to a special voevoda and around him was created the usual *prikaz*. As voevoda they invited one of the most remarkable military captains of that epoch—Prince Dimitry Mikhailovich Pozharsky. He was living not far from Nizhny on his Suzdal estate and was recovering from wounds received before Moscow in the battle with the Poles in the spring of 1611. As "comrades" to Pozharsky were named a Riazan nobleman, Ivan Ivanovich Birkin, who had come to Nizhny "about every agreement and good counsel," and the state secretary Vasily Yudin.

At the same time as Prince Pozharsky was in Nizhny in November, hundreds of servitors whom Sigismund had driven away from Smolensk, Dorogobuzh, and Viazma arrived from Arzamas. Deprived of a settled way of life, these people had been roaming about Russia in search of new pomestie estates for themselves. With alacrity they appeared in Nizhny to serve for public funds as soon as they heard about the levying of an army there. Together with the local Nizhnyite servitors (of whom there were few), they made up the first cadres of the future militia.

Thus was launched that Nizhny Novgorod militia which was destined to create a firm government in the country shattered by the Troubles. In November, 1611, Nizhny had already been joined by the nearest Volga towns, Balakhna and Goro-khovets, and in January by Kazan, Vologda, and the towns of the upper Volga (Yaroslavl and others). Then, at the very beginning of 1612, "they came [to Nizhny] from all towns: the first who came were the Kolomnians, then the Riazanians, then from the Borderland towns came many people and Cossacks and *streltsy* who had sat in Moscow under Tsar Vasily." With astonishing rapidity the movement begun in the city of Nizhny Novgorod expanded into the surrounding region and then became a general movement encompassing the entire northern half of the state. Posad "muzhiks" began it; provincial servitors supported it; a prince of lofty breeding led it; it took on a definite national defensive program—such were the makings that assembled and welded together all those classes of the population which did not want Wladyslaw with his Poles or the Cossacks with their Baby Brigand. The movement united the Russian countryside and set it against the overbearing foes, external and internal alike. Liapunov's attempt was being repeated, but without his fatal mistake of uniting with the mass of "brigand" Cossacks.

Nizhny Novgorod expounded its own program in a special dispatch circulated to the towns at the end of 1611. In it the developments in the movement of the Lower Reaches were revealed and the points of view taken there expressed. Much was said in particular about Cossack "brigandage" and about the desire of the Cossacks to begin "new blood," that is, to renew civil strife by the proclamation of Marina's and her son's claims to the throne. Repudiating the Baby Brigand and the "Lithuanian King," Pozharsky and the Nizhnyites wanted all the land to choose a new sovereign, "whom God shall give us"; but until that time they insisted upon the unity "in one council" of all people from the countryside in order "to go together against the Polish and Lithuanian people," and in order that "the Cossacks shall not disperse the army of the Lower Reaches, as they did before, by their brigandage, plundering, and other brigand enterprises including [the claims of] Marinka's son." Relying on the strength of a united countryside, Pozharsky and the Nizhnyites confidently declared of the Cossacks: "We shall not let them start any trouble; we shall not let the brigands do any evil."

This dispatch produced a powerful impression in all the towns it reached. It was the manifesto of the conservative part of Muscovite society, directed against everything that had diverged from the old Muscovite order. All the supporters of this old order began to be drawn to the Nizhny Novgorod militia. And at the same time the Kremlin inmates—the Poles and the Muscovite "traitors," and the "brigand" Cossacks before Moscow—had to take it into account as their own foe. If the Poles and the boyars starving in the Kremlin siege had to await the outcome of the unavoidable clash between the Nizhnyites and the Cossacks, the Cossack leaders were faced with the immediate need to define their own attitude to the new popular movement. Zarutsky thought to seize Yaroslavl and cross over the Volga so as to cut the communications of Nizhny with the Pomorie and thereby separate the two. The Cossack offensive against Yaroslavl became known to the Nizhnyites, and they took it for the beginning of military operations. Pozharsky accepted Zarutsky's challenge, and the struggle began.

3

According to his initial plan, Pozharsky would have liked to advance with his army directly on Suzdal and Moscow. But the Cossacks' attack on Yaroslavl forced him to alter this intention. It became clear that just as in 1608 the main arena of struggle would be the North. Both sides—the popular movement and the Cossacks—equally comprehended that the North, undevastated by the Troubles, would offer a firm base for whomever mastered it, so both sides aimed to seize it. In the early spring of 1612, Pozharsky swung his forces along the Volga to Yaroslavl, drove the Cossacks out of the town and made it his own firm base, and from there began to send out detachments in various directions to complete the expulsion of the Cossacks from the Pomorie. Zarutsky's well-conceived strategy had failed. The Nizhynites won the Pomorie, and Yaroslavl became the main base of their militia and their governing center, from where Pozharsky did not hasten to move on Moscow.

In actual fact, what could he have done before Moscow? There both his foes held each other in check: the Cossack army was unable either to pry the Poles out of the siege or to leave the walls of the Kremlin and the Walled Town without receiving punishment. By arriving before Moscow, Pozharsky would have risked falling victim, like Liapunov, to a new internal conflict, which had already ruined the popular cause once. By remaining in Yaroslavl, he could calmly wait out events, augment his own army, and consolidate his rear. The newly established popular authority could function most conveniently of all in Yaroslavl, the foremost town of all Zamoskovie and the Pomorie. The central position of Yaroslavl in these regions made it the natural focal point of the united countryside, while its proximity to Moscow gave it strategic importance as well. As a result, during the course of a half-year or five months (March-August, 1612) Yaroslavl played the role of the popular movement's capital and acted as the seat of the provisional government formed in the militia.

When Pozharsky came to Yaroslavl (about April 1, 1612) there was functioning around him a general council, about fifty men in number. In the name of this general council on April 7 a dispatch was sent out to the towns with an invitation to send to Yaroslavl "two men each from all ranks of people and to send with them their counsel with signatures." These town representatives, together with an ecclesiastical sobor and Pozharsky's "general council," were to constitute a council "of all the land." Muscovite Zemsky Sobors were customarily composed of the patriarch's council, the Boyar Duma, and representatives of the countryside. Just such a body "of all the land" was desired in Yaroslavl. But the patriarch's council and the Boyar Duma were nowhere to be found. Patriarch Hermogen had died in February, 1612, in a Moscow prison; the boyars were sitting with the Poles under siege. In Yaroslavl the leaders of the militia were content to convene an ecclesiastical sobor from the clergy there present, headed by Metropolitan Kirill, who had been living in retirement. These were, by the contemporary expression, "the [church] authorities." In Yaroslavl the Boyar Duma appeared in the form of two or three boyars previously there, along with the commanders of the separate divisions of the popular army. According to the contemporary expression, these were "the boyars and the commanders." Representatives of the countryside from the towns were added to the church authorities and the boyars, and by such means was formed a council "of all the land," which conducted the most important affairs—military, judicial, even diplomatic. To Russians and foreigners alike, this council represented a regular and sovereign popular assembly. In dealing with it, the Swedes recognized it as the legitimate power and called it *die Musscowitischen Stände, die Reussischen Stände.* The Russian chronicler and Russian official acts consider it the supreme government "of all the land."

With the aid of this council and under its authority Pozharsky achieved extremely important results in Yaroslavl. The North was cleared of the Cossacks and passed entirely into the hands of the popular army. Although the Swedish government held Novgorod, it promised Pozharsky its neutrality on the condition that in due course, when it came time to elect a tsar, the leaders in Yaroslavl would present the candidacy of Prince Philipp of Sweden for the Muscovite throne. This candidacy had already been accepted by Novgorod, which under Swedish occupation had entered into a forced union with Sweden. Pozharsky himself apparently took Philipp's candidacy seriously; nevertheless, it was looked upon primarily as a means to insure the rear of the Yaroslavl army against a Swedish attack during the advance on Moscow. Besides military and diplomatic affairs, the Yaroslavl authorities actively engaged in building up and provisioning the militia itself. There is reason to think that the Yaroslavl forces were transformed into a powerful and well-organized army, welded together and well trained. Their military superiority over the Cossacks had become manifest to everyone by the close of the summer of 1612.

In Yaroslavl it also behooved Pozharsky and his associates, without awaiting the liberation of Moscow, to elect a tsar. But the matter did not get that far; circumstances forced them toward Moscow earlier than had been anticipated. News was received of Hetman Chodkiewicz's approach to Moscow from Smolensk with Polish forces and provisions for the Moscow garrison. Despite their hostility to the Yaroslavl government, Trubetskoi and Zarutsky informed it of the danger, and Pozharsky immediately advanced on Moscow in order to prevent Chodkiewicz from entering the Kremlin.

4

In August, 1612, a meeting took place before Moscow between the popular army and the Cossack "encampments." It proved fatal for the Cossacks. Approaching Moscow, the Yaroslavl forces kept apart from the Cossacks in fortified strongholds and displayed no desire to draw close to them, for they had resolved "by no means to stand together with the Cossacks." This conduct on the part of the popular army forced the Cossacks to consider whether the Yaroslavl authorities might not have some design against them. A schism developed among the Cossacks which led to the disintegration of their powerful center—the "encampments." In the encampments at that time there were up to 5,000 Cossacks alone, not counting military men of other ranks and designations (like "fighting men from the Borderland towns"); and in addition "before Moscow among all regiments were living Muscovites—trading and manufacturing and every sort of 'black people,' who feed themselves and have all sorts of edible provisions." This nest now fell into complete disorder. Part of its forces immediately placed themselves at Pozharsky's disposal. Another part, not quite half the army, went off to Kolomna under Zarutsky's leadership and from there into the Riazan area and farther south. The remainder did not know what to do or how to conduct themselves vis-à-vis the Yaroslavl army, since it was not coming for union and reconciliation. They no longer had the strength to fight that army; it only remained to wait and to "maintain animosity" against the popular forces because they "do not come to them in the encampments."

About August 20, 1612, Chodkiewicz appeared before Moscow and attacked Pozharsky's forces. After significant vacillation the Cossacks aided Pozharsky, and Chodkiewicz, having sustained great losses, left without reaching the Kremlin. Yet this victory over the common enemy did not reconcile the Russian people, and among the Cossacks some still clung to the idea of "pillaging all the fighting men and driving them away from Moscow." The encampments needed several more weeks before they completely abandoned the idea of a struggle against the popular army and decided to surrender. At the beginning of October, 1612, an agreement was reached between Pozharsky and Trubetskoi: "Upon the petition and compact of all ranks of people, they and the elected man Kuzma Minin stood into unity and bound themselves to accede to the Muscovite State and to wish good to the Russian state in everything, without any cunning designs." A united provisional government was formed in which Trubetskoi's boyar rank gave him titular primacy, whereas actual power belonged to the "council of all the land" and to its Yaroslavl leaders. If there was not much internal agreement in this "unity," the cessation of discord nevertheless bore its own fruit.

On October 22, 1612, the combined forces of the popular militia and the Cossacks took the Walled Town, and four days later the Kremlin also capitulated. The Polish garrison had displayed great heroism during its year-and-a-half confinement in the Kremlin. It had experienced extreme need, extending, it was said, even to cannibalism; it had requested aid many times from its king and had patiently waited for it. But Sigismund, rich neither in forces nor means, could not or would not support it, and Polish dominion in Moscow fell. Sigismund's attempt to return to Moscow in December, 1612, proved abortive because on this occasion, too, the king lacked sufficient forces to storm Moscow's fortifications.

IV

The provisional government chooses a tsar.
1. The convocation of a Zemsky Sobor; its composition.
2. The course of election discussions at the Sobor.
3. The candidacy of Mikhail Feodorovich Romanov and his election.

1

The position of the provisional government after the liberation of Moscow was not an easy one. The Cossacks were incapable of maintaining discipline and threatened constant disturbances and internal dissension over the division of booty and captives. In the Kremlin the siege had produced terrible disorder, which needed to be cleared in a hurry so as to bring Moscow's fortifications into battle readiness. The fighting men of the Yaroslavl militia, who had made a protracted military campaign, had to be released home; yet at the same time the provisional government had to avoid weakening the Moscow garrison, especially in view of Sigismund's impending campaign. Just as pressing was the need to reinforce the success already achieved by electing a tsar and thereby converting the provisional government into a permanent, normal authority.

In the very first weeks after the clearing of the Kremlin, dispatches were sent out from Moscow with a summons for deputies from the towns to elect a tsar. They were expected in Moscow by St. Nicholas's Day (December 6); if that were impossible, they should hurry to arrive by Christmas. They were requested to select "from the sobor (that is, the clergy) and from the posad people, and from the district, from the 'black' rural districts," ten men "of the best and most reasonable and constant people" and to give them "complete and firm and sufficient instruction." They were to speak "about the affairs of state freely and fearlessly" and to be "straightforward, without any cunning designs." In expectation of the deputies' arrival the fighting men were released home from Moscow and the army was demobilized; so by December there was no longer a Yaroslavl army in the capital. "The gentry and *deti boyarskie* dispersed to their pomestie estates, but in Moscow remained gentry and *deti boyarskie* in all two thousand, and of Cossacks nearly five thousand men (4,500), and the *streltsy* with a thousand men, and the peasant-rabble." Such was the garrison with which Moscow was prepared to meet Sigismund in December, 1612.

At the beginning of January, 1613, elected delegates began to assemble in Moscow for the election Sobor. It is impossible to determine how many came in all, since an exact and full list of Sobor participants has not been preserved. Two manuscript copies of the solemn "election charter" or Sobor protocol have come down to us. Under one 235 electors are signed, under the other 238; whereas in all of these signatures the names of 277 participants are mentioned. But this is not their exact number. One delegate signed the charter for many comrades without listing them by name. Thus there were no less than nineteen deputies from Nizhny Novgorod at the Sobor, yet only five men signed the compact on the one copy and six on the other. It could be, therefore, that the number of electors at the Sobor was much greater than 277. Of provincial delegates alone there can be counted up to 500, if one

assumes that towns sent ten men each, as Pozharsky and Trubetskoi had requested; for no less than fifty towns responded to
their call. For that time such a number was sufficiently great,
the more so as it embraced towns of the most varied areas of
the state, from the White Sea to the Don and the Donets. In its
territorial aspect the breakdown of representation at the Sobor
of 1613 was sufficiently full. In its class aspect it was likewise
complete: both the service and the taxpaying classes were represented, and there were representatives of the free Cossacks as
well. As a whole, of course, the Sobor proved to be the organ
of those strata of the Muscovite population that had taken part
in the deliverance of Moscow and the restoration of order in
the country. It could serve neither the adherents of Sigismund
nor the "brigandlike" tendency of the free Cossacks. However,
there were evidently supporters of Sigismund at the Sobor, and
likewise persons who generally favored the election of a foreign
prince. Consequently the course of election discussions at the
Sobor was involved and turbulent. Contemporaries obscurely
relate that "for many days there were gatherings of people, but
they were unable to settle matters and everything wavers back
and forth." "Many were the agitations of people, each wanted
to act according to his own thinking."

2

The first decision which the Sobor announced officially
was the rejection of any foreign candidacy; it was solemnly en-
acted "not to choose the Lithuanian or Swedish king or
their children, for their many injustices, nor to choose people
of the several other lands for the Muscovite State, and not to
desire Marinka and her son." It is not known exactly who proposed a foreigner for tsar. In Yaroslavl very serious negotiations had been going on relative to the Swedish prince, and it
could be that Pozharsky entertained the possibility of selecting
him. To Sigismund and Wladyslaw it was reported in December, 1612, that "there is in Moscow, among the boyars who

served you, Great Sovereign, and among the best people, the desire to request you as ruler, Great Sovereign, Crown Prince Wladyslaw Zhigimontovich." There is also some indication that several Muscovites toyed with the possibility of inviting one of the Hapsburgs to the Muscovite throne. All these considerations and aspirations concerning foreigners were cut short by the Sobor, however, and in mentioning this, one contemporary expressed himself as follows: "The commanders in the meantime wanted for themselves a tsar from the heretics, but the popular military forces did not want this to be." That is, the higher strata of electors were ready to summon a foreigner, but the lower obstructed it. Be that as it may, the question of foreign candidates was withdrawn, and "Marinka and her son" were opportunely repudiated as well. As a consequence, the possibility of a resurgence of pretenders' offspring was virtually destroyed.

Having disposed of this matter, the delegates began to discuss things further: "They were talking at the Sobor about tsareviches who serve in the Muscovite State, and about great families, whom from among them will God grant to the Muscovite State as sovereign." That is, they reviewed the Russified posterity of Tatar and mountain (from the Caucasus) princes and of their own, Muscovite boyars. The most difficult moment of the election session had arrived; it was not easy to decide which of the great families could be turned into a dynasty. The side of the princes had been completely shattered by the Troubles, and their leaders, the Shuiskys and Vasily Golitsyn, were outside the borders of the state in captivity with the king; the remainder, for "service" to Wladyslaw and for sitting with the Poles in the Kremlin siege, were considered traitors. The other faction of the court aristocracy was in no better position. The Godunov family had fallen completely after the death of Boris. The Sheremetievs had been dispersed among all camps and parties. The Romanovs had likewise experienced a difficult time. Their chief and single talented representative, Filaret, was in captivity in Poland; the remainder were insignificant by themselves and in disarray. No one from the great families could be considered the most eminent and most worthy candidate for the throne. Furthermore, after the siege of Moscow the greatest boyars had left the capital, fleeing the false position into which they had fallen. They were not "let into the Duma" —that is, they were debarred from participation in the provisional government of Pozharsky and Trubetskoi—and "they even wrote about them to the towns to all sorts of people: should they be allowed into the Duma or not?" How this question was resolved is not known, but as a result there were no boyars either at the Sobor or in Moscow. They dispersed to their patrimonial estates, turning up in the towns.

In their place, life brought forth new rulers—Pozharsky and the other heads of the popular army and leaders of the provisional government. It is difficult to explain why they did not themselves become aspirants for the throne; yet it is obvious that their influence upon the Sobor was not significant. It was said above that they were inclined to summon a foreigner, but in this they diverged from the bulk of the ordinary electors and had to yield to the latter. Under such conditions it is understandable that the opinions of the electors were divided and that each wanted "to act according to his own thinking." An electioneering fever set in with the usual accompaniments— agitation and bribery. "Many of the grandees who desire to be tsar are bribing, and to many they both give and promise many gifts."

Finally, on February 7, 1613, the Sobor elected as tsar the son of Filaret Romanov, Mikhail Feodorovich. The Troubles had taught the Muscovite people to be cautious; so the Sobor put off the proclamation of its completed election for two weeks—until February 21. First of all, during these two weeks "they sent to the towns of the Muscovite State for boyars, for Prince Feodor Mstislavsky and his comrades, that for the great affair of state and for general counsel of the land they should come to Moscow with dispatch." And second, "to all towns of the Russian tsardom, save the most remote towns, true and

God-fearing men were secretly sent among all people to discover their thoughts about the selection of a ruler, whom they want as sovereign tsar in the Muscovite State in all the towns." And only then, when those sent to the towns had returned with good news and the boyars had assembled in Moscow, was Mikhail Romanov proclaimed tsar on February 21 in the great Moscow palace, which was still not fully restored after the two-year Polish occupation.

3

It is not difficult to understand why, after much vacillation, the Sobor settled upon precisely Mikhail Feodorovich Romanov. To be sure, at first glance his candidacy seems strange. Very young, not yet twenty years old; sickly, because "affected in the legs" from the consequences of a contusion; quiet and inactive—he was "not built" for the well-being of the state. He was deprived of good guidance, since his father was languishing in captivity beyond the borders of Russia, while his lone uncle, Ivan Nikitich, was insignificant in capacities and a man crippled by paralysis. Among the more distant kin of Mikhail there were no capable or worthy people, save perhaps Feodor Ivanovich Sheremetiev, an eminent and respected boyar of that time. How was it possible to summon such a candidate to the throne?

Yet the more closely we look into the circumstances of the moment, the more clearly we shall understand that Mikhail Feodorovich was the single figure around whom both sides of the still not finally reconciled segments of Muscovite society—the service class of the countryside and the Cossacks—could unite. One must remember that the election campaign proceeded under the pressure of the Moscow garrison, in which the Cossacks numerically predominated. Their numbers and their consciousness of power made them dangerous. They did not obey authority: "In everything the Cossacks are more powerful than the boyars and the gentry, they do what they want," observes a contemporary. As early as December, 1612, the Cossacks in Moscow had been discussing the tsar's election, "in order to choose one of the Russian boyars, and they are comparing Filaret's son and the Brigand of Kaluga's son." So, at the very start of the Sobor session Mikhail's candidacy was presented by the Cossack side, along with the candidacy of the Baby Brigand. The latter, of course, the popular forces could not accept, and the moral authority of the Sobor did not permit its consideration; it was dispensed with immediately after the opening of Sobor sessions, together with the candidacies of "heretics." Yet the more decisively the popular forces opposed the Baby Brigand,[28] the more attentively they had to consider the other Cossack candidate.

There can be no doubt that the Cossacks put forward Mikhail, "Filaret's son," from Tushinite memories, for Filaret's name had been closely connected with the Tushino encampments. But the family name of the Romanovs was connected with still another series of Muscovite recollections. From this family had come the first wife of Ivan the Terrible, Anastasia Romanova, "the little dove," whose name was recalled with sympathy and respect. Her brother Nikita Romanovich had enjoyed rare popularity in the time of Ivan the Terrible as a capable administrator, one who had not served in the oprichnina, and a humane person. His name was celebrated in popular and Cossack songs as a friend and protector of the oppressed. The last tsar of the extinct Muscovite dynasty, Feodor Ivanovich, the son of Anastasia, had belonged through his mother to the same Romanov family. Quite independently of the Cossacks, in 1610, when after Shuisky's overthrow there had been talk in Moscow about recognizing Wladyslaw, several segments of the Muscovite population had considered Mikhail Feodorovich Romanov a better candidate for the tsardom than Wladyslaw. In this way Mikhail's candidacy, proposed by the

---

28. "Tsarina" Marina and her young son were captured in 1614; the boy was hanged in Moscow and his mother died in prison soon afterwards. (T.)

Cossacks even prior to the Sobor, assumed a national significance at the Sobor itself; and when it became clear that besides Mikhail there were no other names that could combine the desires of the Cossacks and of the other classes of the population, he was elected.

His election had this significance: it pacified at the most sensitive point two still not completely reconciled social forces and provided them an opportunity for reconciliation and further joint work. This is why the rejoicing of both sides upon the occasion of the agreement reached was sincere and great, and why Muscovites were right when they wrote that Mikhail was chosen "by a unanimous and irrevocable council" of his future subjects.

So the affair seemed to the election Sobor. However, outside observers—Russians and foreigners alike—noted one feature in the course of the tsar's election that is not mentioned either in the election charter or in the other official documents concerning the election. Russian sources have preserved several hints that the Sobor did not itself originate the idea of Mikhail's election, but was led to it by outside pressure, by intervention from the side. There is the story, for example, about how some "renowned ataman of the Don" came to a session of the Sobor and explained Mikhail's rights to the throne. There is another tale that Cossacks, together with gentry, came to the Trinity monk Avraamy Palitsyn at the monastery's chapel in Moscow with a request that he report to the Sobor their thoughts concerning Mikhail's election. These rather vague reports contain sufficiently delicate hints about Cossack influence in Moscow: namely, that the first thought about Mikhail belonged precisely to the Cossacks. From the Poles came not only delicate hints, but direct assertions. In an official explanation of Polish diplomats with the Muscovites in the period immediately after Mikhail's election, it fell to the latter to hear "unflattering words." Leo Sapieha rudely informed Filaret in the presence of the Muscovite envoy that "Don Cossacks alone had set up his son in the Muscovite State as sovereign." And Gosiewski told Prince Vorotynsky that Mikhail had been "chosen only by the Cossacks." In the sharp squabbles between envoys there resounded such words as "Romanov the Cossack Tsar." Like the Poles, the Swedes voiced the same conviction that at Mikhail's election in Moscow everything had been done under Cossack pressure. Studying these impressions of foreigners, the historian must not forget that the role of the Cossacks in the tsar's election was not hidden from the Muscovite people, either, but that it seemed different to them than to foreigners. The tsar's election, which pacified the Troubles and quieted the country, seemed to the popular side the special beneficence of the Lord, and to ascribe to the Cossacks the election of him whom "God himself had revealed" was in their eyes an unseemly absurdity.

Chapter

THE
CONSEQUENCES
OF
THE TROUBLES

I

1. The basis of the new authority—the middle classes. The replacement of the ruling class: the fall of the boyars and the successes of the service gentry. The connection created by the Troubles between the service gentry and the posad population. The defeat of the Cossacks. 2. The Troubles facilitate the growth of political consciousness and independent activity in Muscovite society. The local councils at the Time of Troubles and "all the land."
3. Cultural innovations and foreign policy after the Troubles.

1

The election of Mikhail Feodorovich Romanov is usually considered the end of the Troubles. For the new tsar of Muscovy there remained only the struggle with the consequences of the catastrophe through which the state had passed and with the last, already weak outbursts of sharp social discontent. The leaders of Nizhny Novgorod had liquidated the social struggle. After the defeat and destruction of the boyar government of 1610 and the collapse of Liapunov's service-gentry government of 1611, the initiative had passed to the "last people" (as one contemporary put it), and the initiative of these last Muscovite people, the "burdened" posad people of Nizhny Novgorod, had led to decisive success.

In order of class hierarchy the various classes of Muscovite society had successively taken up the cause of state restoration, and victory had gone to the weakest of them. The boyars, with their rich experience in government, their pride in their "pedigree" and "overflowing wealth," had fallen because of their incautious alliance with an enemy of an alien faith, in union with whom they had sought a way out of the domestic turmoil. The landowning service class, though they wielded military organization, had met unexpected defeat at the hands of the domestic foe, in alliance with whom they had wished to throw off the foreign yoke. At the start of their own movement the posad people of Nizhny had been strong only through bitter political experience, as they had learned from the examples of others to fear unfaithful allies more than declared enemies. They had warily drawn into their own alliance only those social elements that represented the conservative core of Muscovite society. These were the service gentry of middle and minor stature who had not been carried away into "treason" or "brigandage," and the taxpaying "muzhiks" from the urban and rural communes of the northern half of the state, the area least shattered by the crisis of the sixteenth century and by the Troubles of recent years.

This was the social middle, which was attracted neither by the reactionary plans of the princely boyars nor by that searching after a social revolution which had aroused the enserfed mass of peasants and slaves. Declaring open war on "brigand" Cossacks, naming "traitors" all those who cooperated with the Poles, the leaders of the militia of 1612 had also displayed great flexibility and patience in the organization of their relations. Their cautiousness did not degenerate into blind intolerance, and all those who accepted their program and did not arouse their suspicions had received their recognition and good will. The Cossack who wanted to become a service Cossack on state pay, or the Tushinite, even Lithuanian, Pole, or other foreigner who entered popular service "for the house of the most sacred Virgin,"[29] had met no rejection and had joined the ranks of the militia. These ranks had served as a refuge for all who wanted to cooperate in the restoration of the national social structure. Just this definition of program,

---

29. That is, the Cathedral of the Assumption in the Moscow Kremlin. (T.)

together with its broad comprehensiveness, had secured success for the militia of 1612 and had gradually turned its commanders into a stable and firm state authority. Having adopted this program and relying upon the created strength of the middle classes of the population, Tsar Mikhail was kept on the throne and was able to enforce order and to lay the foundation of a new dynasty.

The consequences of the Troubles which the Muscovite State had passed through were very diverse. The class struggle, proceeding protractedly and persistently, had not led to a revolutionary change in social relationships. The intervention of foreign states into this struggle had not destroyed the national independence of Muscovy. Yet both the internal structure of Muscovite society and the external relations of Muscovy suffered profound changes. In vain N. I. Kostomarov, I. E. Zabelin, and other historians have supposed that the Troubles changed nothing in the course of Muscovite history and that, in the final analysis, Muscovite life returned to its old channel, "as it had been under previous sovereigns." The Troubles made Muscovite life different in many respects.

First of all, the Troubles finally destroyed the centuries-old Muscovite aristocracy that had not been finished off by Ivan the Terrible. Embittered by his persecutions, the princes had nevertheless survived Ivan and had witnessed the end of his dynasty. They held for their own the right to succeed it and, having destroyed the Godunovs, had raised to the throne their own leader, Prince Vasily Shuisky. However, the turmoil proved to be more powerful than the boyar oligarchy and destroyed Shuisky. Then the boyars had rushed into union with the Polish Commonwealth and, having fallen into onerous Polish servitude, appeared to be "traitors" and thereby forfeited all moral credit and political power. In Yaroslavl a new government was organized without them; in Moscow a new dynasty was created without them. Those few great princely families that had not died out during the oprichnina and the Troubles became emaciated and impoverished in the seventeenth century; having pushed them aside, the new dynasty created around itself a new aristocracy, a court-bureaucratic nobility with great holdings of both land and money. In order to make a career, the old princes had to travel the same route of faithful service and court favor by which the other careerists of the seventeenth century went, who declared that "the Sovereign is like God: and he makes the lesser great."

Also changed, thanks to the Troubles, was the position of the service class—the gentry and *deti boyarskie,* the pomeshchiks of the grand sovereign. In the sixteenth century the government had actively settled these pomeshchiks on service lands, binding peasant labor to them by every means and striving to see that they served in good order. With this aim the gentry of each district had been organized into a military unit, a "town," and these towns were headed by elected gentry "assessors" who were obligated to keep an account of all gentry of the district. Of course, this was a certain measure of organization, but it existed not for self-government and not in the interests of the gentry themselves. Apart from the service tie they were isolated and led lonely lives on their pomestie estates. In the turmoil, when government influence had weakened while this or that foe suddenly descended upon a district in the form of a Polish detachment or Cossack band, the gentry were unable to meet the danger together in a group. Separately they saved themselves in the forests or rushed to the nearest town and there sat it out along with the urban taxpaying population. Only by relying upon posad "muzhiks," by feeding on urban provisions, and by using urban "outfittings" (cannon) had they been converted into a well-organized army and become powerful. In the Troubles this frequently occurred. The general danger drew together and linked the separate social classes, and by fusing them together in the Yaroslavl militia as a popular army, it finally united them in a strong alliance of the middle classes.

And this alliance emerged the victor in the social struggle. It liberated Moscow; it created the government of Pozharsky; it filled the Zemsky Sobor of 1612-1613 with its representatives; and finally, having chosen a tsar, it formed around him a firm support for his authority. From the midst of this alliance came the leading figures of the new Muscovite administration: the urban voevoda; the *prikaz* "judge" [administrator]; the *prikaz* secretary who administered the state treasury and state domains; the trading man—the great merchant or lesser guild merchant. Two or three decades after its initial victory in 1612 this new nobility already felt its own strength and presented the government with a series of insistent petitions—in extremely respectful form, to be sure—for the satisfaction of its class needs; while in 1648 it stepped forth, correctly again but already less respectfully, with a demand for legislative reform. The Englishman Giles Fletcher had been right when in 1591 he had predicted that victory in the Muscovite civil conflict would go not to the aristocracy nor to the mass of the people, but to the social middle—to the army ("the militarie forces").

As the social middle succeeded, so the social depths, which during the Troubles had operated under the names of the Cossacks and the "brigands," lost. They had succeeded by three blows (in 1606, 1608, and 1611) in shattering and toppling the "boyar" state order and even—for a brief instant—in seizing the governing apparatus. But in place of the structure of life they had destroyed, they brought forth nothing new either in idea or in practical form. They were a destructive force, but completely uncreative, and for the neutral social elements of the countryside they offered nothing that might have tempted the latter in favor of the Cossacks against the boyars. In consequence, "all the land" opposed the Cossacks and declared war on them. In 1612 it defeated them decisively. From before Moscow that part of the Cossacks who did not want to capitulate to the popular militia of the countryside went off to the Don and then to the Caspian. The more radical of them, having lost all hope of conquering Russia, negotiated with the shah of Persia about becoming subjects; but before this could be consummated they were defeated by Muscovite armies and their leader, Zarutsky, was executed. Other circles of Cossacks established themselves on the Don in the form of a unique association, with an elected authority ("elders") at their head.

Meanwhile, those Cossacks who had joined Pozharsky before Moscow and who comprised the Moscow garrison were gradually dispersed among various services. Finally, the remnant of "brigand" Cossacks who continued outlaw operations around Moscow and in Russia generally were mercilessly exterminated. "Brigand" Cossacks ceased to exist. But since the bondage system in the state continued to weigh upon the laboring mass, flight from serf estates also continued. Runaways now went to the Don and "filled the river," but in the course of a whole half-century the idea of "shaking up Moscow" did not arise. This aim only cropped up again in the time of the notorious Stenka Razin.[30]

As a result, the Troubles did not change the social structure of Muscovy, but they did shift its center of gravity from the boyars to the service gentry. A change of governing class took place, and the new governing class reserved in the future the right to peasant and slave labor, as well as the right to court and service careers. It appeared as the full-fledged heir to the previous "high-born" princes and boyars "of the Sovereigns of all the Russian lands," who in the Troubles had met their political end.

2

The Troubles likewise brought about profound changes in the sphere of Muscovite political conceptions and relationships. Prior to the disturbances the Muscovite State of the sixteenth century had been viewed as the "patrimony" of the tsar and grand prince. Muscovite sovereigns had taken the full measure of the ancient appanage prince's proprietary rights to

---

30. Cossack leader of an unsuccessful revolt against Muscovy in the middle Don and the lower Volga regions in 1669-1671. (T.)

his hereditary appanage and had extended them over the whole state. The population of this patrimony were not seen as citizens of their country, but were considered either "servants" and "slaves" of their proprietor-sovereign or his "pilgrims" and "orphans," who ran their own economy "on the land of the sovereign, but in their own settlement." Muscovites were unable to think of their country otherwise than as a "house" which had its owner and master, or "mighty one" [*sil'nozhitel'*] as one Muscovite writer expressed it. When this "mighty one" died or when the Muscovite dynasty was cut short, the "house" remained without a head and proprietor and was devastated by "home-nurtured" slaves. Arch-conservative Muscovites conceived the Troubles precisely as the wilfulness of slaves in an escheated estate. Still, the shattering events of the Troubles and the necessity of organizing the house without a "master" forced Muscovite minds to recover their sight and to comprehend that a country without a sovereign is still a state, that "slaves" are essentially citizens, and that they themselves had a duty to organize and to guard their own community.

When the old ties that had united the regions in common subordination to Moscow were broken, and amidst the turmoil the general state structure had fallen apart, local ties assumed great significance. In the absence of agents from the central government the agents of self-government became the real authority. Governing arrangements were replaced by the decisions of local *"mirs."* Whole regions began to live by the agreements of such *"mirs,"* which according to proximity entered into constant relations with one another. These relations or "circulations" even went on between towns distant from each other. Usually they proceeded as follows: the various estate organizations of a town or rural district set up an all-town or all-district council, and in the name of the town or rural district this council entered into correspondence with other towns and summoned envoys from them or sent its own to them. In 1611 this custom of sending emissaries of the populace to other towns "for good counsel" became especially widespread. For example, the well-known Riazan voevoda Liapunov sent the nobleman Birkin with a state secretary, gentry, and people of every rank to Nizhny "for a treaty," and sent his own nephew with noblemen to Kaluga. From Kazan a lesser servitor, two *streltsy*, and a posad man traveled as envoys to Viatka. The town of Perm dispatched two messengers to Ustiug "for counsel about the cross-kissing and about news." The gentry sent one nobleman from Galich to Kostroma "for good counsel," while the posad people sent one representative. From Yaroslavl, "from all the town," a nobleman and a posad man were sent to Vologda. The town of Vladimir dispatched gentry and "the best" posad people to Suzdal "for counsel."

In short, sending representatives elected by the local communes from one town to another became a custom, and the union of the representatives of several regions into one all-class "council" happened as a natural consequence of the exceptional events of the Troubled Epoch. The local self-governing commune with its elected "communal office" served as the foundation on which first an all-class council "of all the town" sprang up, and then a council of several towns, organized by delegates from all strata of the free population; that is, the clergy, the gentry, and the "burdened" people.

Upon this same foundation grew up the elected "council of all the land," at that moment when the councillors from the towns first united into a Sobor embracing the entire countryside and began to consider themselves the supreme authority in the country. This came about during the most extreme "ruin," when the Muscovite State seemed completely devastated by external conquest and internal conflict. At that time, in a desperate lunge the "last" Muscovites were roused for their homeland, succeeded in uniting into the general militia of 1612, and from the forms of local elective representation familiar to them created an elective "council of all the land." Not having any other authority besides the one elected, these "last people" transferred supreme leadership in the affairs of the whole country to their own elected council.

Thus in the terrible turmoil was born "all the land"—the sovereign council of elected men from the countryside that considered itself the supreme arbiter of affairs and the master of the country. Alongside the old concept of the "sovereign tsar and grand prince of all Russia" developed the new conception of "all the land," personified in its delegates. Alongside the great "sovereign's affairs" stood the "great affair of the land." For the new tsar elected by "all the land," the tsardom could never become simply a "patrimony," because his family had no patrimonial rights to the state. The new tsar had received authority not over a private estate, but over a people who had been able to organize themselves and to create their own provisional authority in "all the land." It fell to the permanent authority which had sprung up in the person of the new sovereign to define its relations to "all the land" and to rule in conjunction with the latter. The ancient patrimonial-state order yielded place to a new, higher and more complex one—the nation-state. Moreover, the new authority had to operate in accordance with new conditions.

In the initial days of his reign Tsar Mikhail Feodorovich found himself in a difficult position: internal chaos still continued; external foes threatened as before; the treasury was empty. The Zemsky Sobor, having elected the tsar, employed all efforts to restore order, to collect forces and funds. But this could not be done at once, and the young sovereign reproachfully pointed out the disorganization to the Sobor, threatening not to accept the proffered authority and even vacillating about whether to go to the capital. He saw no possibility of ruling the country and pacifying the "universal revolt" without the cooperation of the Sobor, and he demanded this cooperation, calling upon "all the land" to assist in all matters of government. Putting it differently, at first the new sovereign wanted to rule together with the Sobor and did not view this as a diminution of his own autocratic rights and power. For its part, "all the land" did not in the least desire to diminish the authority of its own representative, and with obedient zeal it went to his aid in everything that it could.

The tsar elected by the "land" and the popular assembly not only did not dispute each other's rights and primacy, but firmly supported one another in the same concern for their common safety and security. Consciousness of a common weal and mutual dependence led the central authority and its council of "all the land" to the fullest agreement, and converted the tsar and "all the land" into one indivisible political force, which struggled with currents hostile to it within and without the state. Thus the circumstances of the Troubled Time gave a complex structure to the Muscovite constitution; it was composed of the personal authority of an unlimited sovereign and the collective authority of a Sobor of "all the land." Every "affair of the great sovereign and of the land" was resolved at that time "by the decree of the great sovereign and by the compact of all the land." The sovereign's decree, moreover, willingly relied upon the "compact of the land," whereas the "compact of the land" received force only by the sovereign's order. No charters existed that might have defined this interrelationship of the central authority and the popular representation, and there is no possibility of speaking about a "limitation" of Mikhail Feodorovich's authority. Nevertheless, the close connection between the tsar and "all the land" and the collective character of the state authority under Tsar Mikhail stand beyond doubt.

In the first decade of Mikhail Feodorovich's reign the Zemsky Sobor apparently functioned in Moscow without interruption, and "all the land" was always near its sovereign. In the remaining period of Mikhail's life Sobors were summoned with extraordinary frequency, though it is no longer possible to speak of their continuity. Pacification was completed within the state, and stabilization achieved on the borders. The disturbed times were over, and society settled back into peace. For the autocracy there was no longer the constant necessity to seek the opinion of "all the land" and to rely upon its "compact." Under the son of Mikhail Feodorovich, Tsar Alexis [reigned, 1645-1676], the *prikaz* principle—that is, bureaucracy —increasingly prevailed in the system of administration. Sobors were summoned with diminishing frequency, and "all the land" gradually became not the administrator but an administered ward of the state. Yet for a long time Muscovites still recalled the deeds of "all the land" and believed that without it there was no salvation amidst dangers. As soon as any kind of extraordinary state matter cropped up, they indicated that "that matter is a great one of all the land of all the state"; "that is a matter of all the state—of all the towns and of all ranks." From the grand sovereign they would "request the favor" that he "order in that matter to take from all the ranks in Moscow and from the towns the best people. . . ." Thus they talked in 1662-1663, for example, during the famine and financial difficulties in the Muscovite State.

3

Beyond social and political innovations the Troubles also introduced cultural novelties into Muscovite life. Before the Troubles only the tsar's court and chance individuals had come into contact with foreigners and seen them in Moscow. Service duties rarely caused Russian envoys or *gosti* (commercial agents) to venture abroad and to observe European life with their own eyes. In the Turbulent Time, however, contact with foreigners became constant and general for Muscovites. In the train of the first pretender there appeared in Moscow hundreds, even thousands of Poles, Lithuanians, and every sort of "German"—military, commercial, and industrial personnel. After suffering in the rioting of 1606, foreigners appeared anew in Tushino and from there wandered about the country in the Tushinite bands. On the other hand, they arrived in Moscow with Skopin-Shuisky in the form of an "armored detachment" of *Landsknechte* (mercenary soldiers); from there they went to Klushino and then back to Novgorod, where they settled for a long time. Intercourse with these newcomers of varied nationalities became an unavoidable necessity for Russians and brought with it, principally, two consequences. First, the Russian people were convinced that for their own needs and profit it was necessary to master European technology. After the Troubles the Muscovite government borrowed extensively from the West in military and every other science. And second, Russians saw that the Lithuanians, Poles, and "Germans" knew how to live more cheerfully and did not fear divine punishment for worldly comforts, since they did not impute sin, necessitating repentance and punishment, to such things. If the first consequence—practical borrowing—was inescapable and was carried out according to the dictates of state service, the second was a matter of personal initiative and taste. European costume, the shaving of beards, music, fanciful objects of home furnishing penetrated into Muscovite life along with the Latin and the Polish book, religious free-thinking, and new political ideas. Seventeenth-century Muscovy experienced an intellectual ferment which carried with it the seeds of that Europeanization of Russia which so broadly emerged under Peter the Great.

Finally, to exhaust completely the list of what should be considered consequences of the Troubles, we should recall the course of Muscovite foreign policy in the seventeenth century. The Muscovite State had come out of the turmoil with the loss of its western regions. Novgorod and other towns of the "German borderland" had been seized by the Swedes; Smolensk and the towns of the "Lithuanian borderland" had been taken by the Poles. Muscovite policy under the new dynasty did not concede these losses for a minute. The Swedes soon gave up Novgorod (1617), leaving them with only the seacoast from the river Narova to the town of Korela. Smolensk, however, continued to be in the possession of the Polish Commonwealth, and furthermore Wladyslaw considered himself to be the legitimate sovereign of Muscovy. All the powers of the Muscovite State were directed toward settling accounts with these foes, and most of all with the Poles. The idea of retribution lived on in Muscovite hearts independently of the desire to regain the lost lands. All the wars of the seventeenth century were conducted with this idea of retribution, and only in 1686 was "eternal peace" achieved with the Polish Commonwealth instead of temporary truces; while only under Peter the Great were final accounts settled with Sweden. The constant military expenditures for the support and conduct of these wars pressed upon the population in the most burdensome fashion and ruined the state. But Muscovites were unable to abandon accounts with those who in the Troubles had done Muscovy "much injustice," just as they could not reconcile themselves to the loss of the seacoast and of free intercourse with the Baltic ports. The sea insistently beckoned to all Muscovite statesmen of the seventeenth century.

Translator's Appendices

Genealogical Chart

THE MUSCOVITE HOUSE OF RURIK

Ivan III
(1440-1505; ruled 1462-1505)

Vasily III
(1479-1533; ruled 1505-1533)

Anastasia Romanovna ——— Ivan IV ——— Maria Nagoi
(d. 1560)   *(1530-1584; ruled 1547-1584)*   *(his seventh wife)*

Feodor Ivanovich ——— Irina Godunov   Dimitry
(1557-1598)   *(d. 1603)*   *(ca. 1582-1591)*

Feodosia
(died an infant in 1593)

THE GODUNOVS

Maria Skuratova ——————————— Boris Feodorovich Godunov
(murdered 1606)   *(ca. 1551-1605; ruled 1598-1605)*

Ksenia Borisovna   Feodor Borisovich
(158?-1622)   *(ca. 1589-1606; murdered)*

THE ROMANOVS

Roman Yurievich Zakharin

Anastasia Romanovna
(Ivan IV's first wife, d. 1560)

Nikita Romanovich Yuriev-Zakharin
(d. 1585)

Feodor Nikitich Romanov
[Filaret] (d. 1633)

Mikhail Feodorovich Romanov
(ca. 1596-1645; ruled 1613-1645)

Alexis Mikhailovich
(1629-1676; ruled 1645-1676)

Chronological Table

1478 Muscovy annexes Novgorod.

1533-1584 The reign of Ivan IV, the Terrible.

1547-1556 End of regency over Ivan IV; internal reforms: law code of 1550; local government and church reforms; military service based on land—the pomestie system—is regularized; Muscovite expansion to the southeast leads to the conquest of the Tatar khanates of Kazan (1552) and Astrakhan (1556).

1553 Opening of the White Sea route to Muscovy by the Englishman Richard Chancellor.

1558-1583 Ivan the Terrible's unsuccessful Livonian War, which soon developed into war against Poland-Lithuania, and from 1561 against Sweden as well.

1564 First book printed in Moscow.

1565-1572 The oprichnina of Ivan the Terrible.

1569 The Union of Lublin between Poland and Lithuania, forming the Polish-Lithuanian Commonwealth.

1571 Moscow burned by the Crimean Tatars.

1581 Yermak and his Cossacks overthrow the khanate of Siberia, thereby beginning Muscovite expansion east of the Urals. Peasant departure curtailed by the institution of "forbidden years."

1584-1598 The reign of the weakminded Feodor Ivanovich, with Boris Godunov as "Lord Protector" (regent) from 1587.

1585 The foundation of Arkhangelsk (or Archangel).

1591 The mysterious death of "Tsarevich Dimitry," Ivan the Terrible's son by his seventh wife.

1598-1605 The reign of Boris Godunov, elected by the Zemsky Sobor.

1601-1603 Famine; Khlopko's revolt.

1604 The first false Dimitry invades the Seversk Borderland, with Polish-Lithuanian assistance.

1605 Boris Godunov's sudden death leads to the overthrow of his son by a boyar plot, and to the installation of the self-styled "Tsarevich Dimitry" as tsar.

1606 A second boyar plot causes rioting in Moscow, resulting in the the murder of "Tsar Dimitry" and the enthronement of Vasily Shuisky, "the boyar Tsar."

1606-1610 The reign of Vasily Shuisky.

1606-1607 The revolt of Bolotnikov, ending with his defeat by Shuisky's forces.

1608 "The Brigand" (the second false Dimitry) invades Muscovy from Poland and besieges Moscow from nearby Tushino.

1610-1611 Shuisky's near-victory over the Brigand is foiled by the Polish Commonwealth's open intervention into the Muscovite civil war. Polish forces under Hetman Zolkiewski defeat Shuisky's army at Klushino and occupy Moscow (August, 1610); Sigismund III captures Smolensk (June, 1611). Shuisky is deposed, and Sigismund's son Wladyslaw is chosen tsar by the boyars in Moscow. National reaction to Polish domination, but Liapunov's attempt to liberate Moscow fails because of internal social conflict.

1612 Minin and Pozharsky lead a new campaign, begun in Nizhny Novgorod, and with Cossack aid retake Moscow from the Poles.

1613 Mikhail Romanov is elected tsar by the Zemsky Sobor, marking the end of the Time of Troubles and the start of the Romanov dynasty.

Glossary of Terms

Bashkirs—semi-nomadic Turkic people who inhabit the Urals region southeast of Kazan. They came under a vague Muscovite protectorate after the fall of the Kazan Khanate in 1552.

"black lands"—lands directly under the prince's control on which peasant communal self-government was organized under the supervision of agents of the local prince. Such peasants were often termed "black people" or "burdened (i.e., tax-bearing) people."

boyar duma—the grand prince of Muscovy's council of nobles and his chief executive organ of government until its position was weakened by the oprichnina and the Time of Troubles. Its membership was divided into several grades—boyars, *okolnichy*, nobles of the duma, state secretaries. The duma was finally abolished by Peter the Great.

Cheremis (Mari)—Finno-Ugrian people who inhabited areas of northeastern European Russia from very ancient times. Their present area of habitation is roughly between Nizhny Novgorod (now Gorky) and Kazan.

chet' (plural *cheti*)—old measure of land equal to one-half of a *desiatina.*

Cossacks—frontiersmen who as refugees from the Muscovite and Polish-Lithuanian states began to appear in the southern steppe in the fifteenth and sixteenth centuries. Some were organized into self-governing communal societies (on the Dnieper, the Don, and the Yaik [Ural]). These semiautonomous communities conducted independent foreign policies, though they frequently allied with Muscovy. Other Cossacks were simply special categories of Muscovite servitors.

desiatina—land measure equal to two *cheti,* or 2.7 acres or 1.092 hectares.

desiatinnaia land—state-owned land on the borderlands of the Muscovite State on which new colonists were indirectly brought into state service by their obligation to till parcels of this land for the sovereign.

deti boyarskie—"boyar sons," a lower echelon of Muscovite service gentry.

Lobnoe mesto—Place of the Skull, on Red Square before the Kremlin, where public proclamations were read and executions carried out.

mestnichestvo—system that correlated the service position of nobles in Muscovy with the genealogical standing of their ancestors.

Mordvinians—Finno-Ugrian people who inhabit the region along the Sura River, southwest of Kazan.

okolnichy—a rank of service nobility second only to the boyars.

oprichnina—the system introduced by Tsar Ivan the Terrible in 1565 to break the power of his real or supposed domestic foes. The tsar created his own patrimony, the oprichnina, within the regular state, thus subjecting large portions of the country to direct autocratic rule. It lasted officially to 1572.

pomestie estate—land held on condition of rendering military service to the sovereign.

pomeshchik—holder of a pomestie estate, i.e., the service gentry of the Muscovite State.

Pomorie—literally "region along the sea," the northwestern areas of the Muscovite State bordering on the White Sea, the Arctic Ocean, and extending inland along the northern rivers such as the Northern Dvina.

posad—commercial-manufacturing quarter of Muscovite towns (somewhat analogous to *faubourg* in medieval Western Europe), its inhabitants were organized as an urban commune and were subject to taxation by the grand dukes of Muscovy.

posadnik—chief official of early Russian towns, usually appointed by the prince; but in Novgorod from the thirteenth century to the Muscovite conquest in 1478, the *veche* elected the *posadnik,* the archbishop, and other officials.

prikaz—(plural: *prikazy)*—term for an administration or bureau in sixteenth- and seventeenth-century Muscovy, usually headed by a boyar or a state secretary.

Seversk—sometimes translated as Severia, the term refers to a region in the present day northeastern Ukraine centered around the town of Novgorod Seversky (not to be confused with Novgorod the Great in northwestern Russia).

St. George's Day—November 26, the traditional time at which free peasants could migrate to another area. This custom was gradually abrogated in the latter part of the sixteenth century, marking a crucial step toward the final enserfment of the last remaining free elements of the Russian peasantry.

streltsy—(plural of *strelets*)—semi-professional musketeers created by Ivan the Terrible in the middle of the sixteenth century. Organized as untaxed communal groups, the *streltsy* engaged in industry and petty trade in their spare time from service.

veche—town assembly in early Russian towns, it obtained particular power in the city-states of Novgorod and Pskov, but was suppressed upon their annexation by Muscovy.

voevoda—originally military governors, they were centrally appointed heads of government in the towns, responsible to the tsar and to the *prikazy*. The term also simply meant general.

Zamoskovie—literally, "land beyond the Moskva River," the territory north and east of Moscow.

Zemsky Sobor—Assembly of the Land, "All the Land," or a sort of Muscovite estates-general. It grew up in the sixteenth century, but disappeared by the end of the seventeenth century.

For Further Reading

In recent years interest in the pre-1700 period of Russian history has grown substantially; nevertheless, the literature available in English on the subject is still rather sparse. And what is true of the epoch as a whole is even more true of the Time of Troubles in particular. In this essay I shall therefore enumerate a selection of sources, studies, and imaginative works bearing on various topics touched upon by Platonov. With only a few exceptions chronological coverage will be limited to the period 1450-1650.

A. Sources

On the Time of Troubles proper, there are the memoirs of Hetman Stanislas Zolkiewski, *Expedition to Moscow,* J. Giertych, ed. and trans. (London, 1959). Other accounts by eyewitnesses can be found in S. A. Zenkovsky, ed., *Medieval Russia's Epics, Chronicles, and Tales* (New York, 1963), which includes two selections from the works of the monk Avraamy Palitsyn; and in B. Dmytryshyn, ed., *Medieval Russia: A Source Book, 900-1700* (New York, 1967), which prints Konrad Bussow's account of the Russian famine of 1601-1604, a letter from the first pretender to Boris Godunov, and the conditions proposed to Wladyslaw in 1610. R. E. F. Smith, *The Enserfment of the Russian Peasantry* (Cambridge, 1968), provides translated documents concerning the status of the peasantry before, during, and after the Time of Troubles, as does Richard Hellie's broader anthology, *Readings for Introduction to Russian Civilization: Muscovite Society* (Chicago, 1967); the latter is available in multilithed form from the University of Chicago Bookstore. Professor Hellie has provided provocative introductions to each section of translated documents.

Source materials on Muscovy in the sixteenth and seventeenth centuries, exclusive of the Time of Troubles, are somewhat more plentiful. Russian accounts of Ivan the Terrible are well represented by J. L. I. Fennell's masterful editions of *The Correspondence between Prince A. M. Kurbsky and Tsar Ivan IV of Russia, 1564-1579* (Cambridge, 1955) and *Prince A. M. Kurbsky's History of Ivan IV* (Cambridge, 1965). Ivan's will, and those of his Muscovite predecessors, have been made available in translation by Robert C. Howes, ed., *The Testaments of the Grand Princes of Moscow* (Ithaca, N.Y.,

1967). The editor has prefaced his publication with a lengthy introduction that analyzes many aspects of Muscovite history.

Heading the list of foreign accounts is Giles Fletcher's pungent *Of the Russe Common Wealth,* a source that greatly influenced Platonov's interpretation of the period leading to the outbreak of the Troubles. Fletcher's colorful commentary is now available in several recent editions: in Lloyd E. Berry, ed., *The English Works of Giles Fletcher the Elder* (Madison, Wis., 1964), which appends the most complete biography of Fletcher; under its own title in a facsimile edition by John Fine and Richard Pipes (Cambridge, Mass., 1966); in a modernized version by Albert J. Schmidt (Ithaca, N.Y., 1966); and in the older edition by E. A. Bond, *Russia at the Close of the Sixteenth Century* (London, 1856; reprinted New York, 1965), which also includes "The Travels of Sir Jerome Horsey," another important source that Platonov utilized extensively. A convenient edition of six English travelogues, including those by Fletcher and Horsey, is Lloyd E. Berry and Robert O. Crummey, eds., *Rude & Barbarous Kingdom: Russia in the Accounts of Sixteenth-Century English Voyagers* (Madison, Wis., 1968). Of great importance for the history of the oprichnina are the writings of a Westphalian adventurer, Heinrich von Staden, which Thomas Esper has edited and translated as *The Land and Government of Muscovy: A Sixteenth-Century Account* (Stanford, 1967). On Muscovy after the Troubles, see Samuel H. Baron's edition of *The Travels of Olearius in Seventeenth-Century Russia* (Stanford, 1967).

The anthologies by Smith and Hellie listed above contain numerous documents, primarily of a legal character, treating the periods before and after the Troubles. On the earlier period they may be supplemented by Horace W. Dewey, ed. and trans., *Muscovite Judicial Texts, 1488-1556* (Ann Arbor, 1966) [Michigan Slavic Materials, No. 7], available through the Department of Slavic Languages, University of Michigan.

B. Studies

To date there are only four books in English specifically on the Time of Troubles or subphases of the period. They are the recent biography of the first pretender by Philip L. Barbour, *Dimitry* (Boston, 1966); the older account by Prosper Mérimée, *Demetrius the Impostor,* trans. A. R. Scoble (London, 1853); Stephan Graham's study, *Boris Godunov* (New Haven, 1933); and the popularization by Sonia E. Howe, *The False Dmitri* (New York, 1916). None of these is particularly scholarly.

More scholarly treatments of the period can be found in the various surveys of Russian history. The fullest and most recent of these will doubtless be the recently published study by George Vernadsky, *The Tsardom of Moscow, 1547-1682*, 2 vols. (New Haven, 1969) [A History of Russia, vol. V]. A classic account is V. O. Kliuchevsky, *A Course in Russian History: The Seventeenth Century*, trans. N. Dudington (Chicago, 1969). Platonov's own textbook for secondary schools, available in translation as *History of Russia*, ed. F. Golder, trans. E. Aronsberg (New York, 1925; reprinted Bloomington, Ind., 1965), contains a thorough treatment, as do the numerous more recent surveys by American and British academics. Of these latter, perhaps the most original is James H. Billington, *The Icon and the Axe: An Interpretive History of Russian Culture* (New York, 1966). For widely varying Marxist approaches, see M. N. Pokrovsky, *History of Russia from the Earliest Times to the Rise of Commercial Capitalism*, ed. and trans. J. D. Clarkson (New York, 1930; reprinted with a new introduction by J. D. Clarkson, Bloomington, Ind., 1966), and the more recent Soviet work by I. I. Smirnov *et al., A Short History of the USSR*, vol. I (New York, 1965). Concise, up-to-date surveys by specialists are provided in the relevant volumes of *The New Cambridge Modern History* (Cambridge, 1957–). And a very broad treatment is furnished by Francis Dvornik, *The Slavs in European History and Civilization* (New Brunswick, N.J., 1962).

Political theory throughout the Muscovite period is briefly discussed in S. V. Utechin, *Russian Political Thought: A Concise History* (New York, 1964), and somewhat more fully in Thornton Anderson, *Russian Political Thought, An Introduction* (Ithaca, N.Y., 1967). Both books list additional references. On more specialized problems, see Michael Cherniavsky, *Tsar and People: Studies in Russian Myths* (New Haven, 1961; reprinted New York, 1969), and A. V. Soloviev, *Holy Russia: The History of a Religious-Social Idea* (New York, 1959). Church-state relations are studied by William K. Medlin, *Moscow and East Rome* (Geneva, 1952). On Muscovite literature, see the Soviet text by N. K. Gudzy, *History of Early Russian Literature*, trans. S. W. Jones (New York, 1949).

The few specialist articles on the period of the Troubles include: Ervin C. Brody, "The Demetrius Episode in a Drama of Lope de Vega," *Polish Review,* XIII, no. 1 (Winter, 1968), 20-38; A. M. Nikolaieff, "Boris Godunov and the Ouglich Tragedy," *Russian Review,* IX, no. 4 (October, 1950), 275-285; A. H. Thompson, "The Legend of Tsarevich Dimitry: Some Evidence of an Oral Tradition," *Slavonic and East European Review,* XLVI, no. 106 (January, 1968), 48-59; and George Vernadsky, "The Death of Tsarevich Dimitry: A Reconsideration of the Case," *Oxford Slavonic Papers,* V (1954), 1-19, which supports Platonov's interpretation of the affair.

The period preceding the Troubles proper has been the subject of numerous studies, though large gaps still remain to be covered. On the early growth of Muscovy there are two scholarly studies by J. L. I. Fennell, *The Emergence of Moscow, 1304-1359* (Berkeley, 1967), and *Ivan the Great of Moscow* (London, 1961). The latter subject is presented in more popular fashion by Ian Grey, *Ivan III and the Unification of Russia* (London, 1964; New York, 1967). The Muscovite conquest of Novgorod has recently been reevaluated in two articles by Joel Raba: "The Fate of the Novgorodian Republic," *Slavonic and East European Review,* XLV, no. 105 (July, 1967), 307-323, and "Novgorod in the Fifteenth Century: A Re-examination," *Canadian Slavic Studies,* I, no. 3 (Fall, 1967), 348-364. The same subject introduces George Vernadsky's learned volume, *Russia at the Dawn of the Modern Age* (New Haven, 1959) [A History of Russia, vol. IV], which covers Muscovite internal history to the 1530's and extends its treatment of developments in the west Russian lands to the latter part of the sixteenth century. On the early phase of conflict between Muscovy and the Grand Duchy of Lithuania, there is the detailed study by Oswald P. Backus, *Motives of West Russian Nobles in Deserting Lithuania for Moscow, 1377-1514* (Lawrence, Kan., 1957). A major political institution of the era is discussed by Gustave Alef, "Reflections on the Boyar Duma in the Reign of Ivan III," *Slavonic and East European Review,* XLV, no. 104 (January, 1967), 76-123; while another article by the same author, "The Origin and Early Development of the Muscovite Postal Service," *Jahrbücher für Geschichte Osteuropas,* XV, no. 1 (March, 1967), 1-15, qualifies popular notions concerning the alleged backwardness of Muscovite institutions as compared to those of Western Europe.

Ivan the Terrible and his times have long fascinated historians; yet, strangely, no satisfactory biography of the tsar himself nor any detailed, modern study of his reign has yet appeared. More or less popular biographies are proffered by H. Eckardt (New York, 1949), Stephan Graham (New Haven, 1933; reprinted Hamden, Conn., 1968), Ian Grey (London, 1964), Jules Koslow (New York, 1961), A. Pember (London, 1895), and K. Waliszewski (New York, 1904; reprinted Hamden, Conn., 1966); all are entitled *Ivan the Terrible*. Two other popularizations are by Harold Lamb, *The March of Muscovy: Ivan the Terrible and the Growth of the Russian Empire, 1400-1648* (Garden City, N.Y., 1948), and by R. Yu. Wipper in a Stalinist interpretation, *Ivan Groznyi* (third edition in English, Moscow, 1947).

Of the scholarly literature on Ivan, historiographical discussions are presented by G. H. Bolsover, "Ivan the Terrible in Russian Historiography," *Transactions of the Royal Historical Society*, fifth series, VII (1957), 71-89; by Platonov himself under the same title, in S. Harcave, ed., *Readings in Russian History*, vol. I (New York, 1962), 188-194; and by Leo Yaresh in a review of Soviet writing, "Ivan the Terrible and the *Oprichnina*," in C. E. Black, ed., *Rewriting Russian History* (second edition revised, New York, 1962), 216-232. A stimulating recent interpretation is Michael Cherniavsky's "Ivan the Terrible as Renaissance Prince," *Slavic Review*, XXVII, no. 2 (June, 1968), 195-211. Particularly incisive on political theory are two studies by the Danish scholar Bjarne Norretranders: "Ivan Groznyj's Conception of Tsarist Authority," *Scandoslavica*, IX (1963), 238-248, and *The Shaping of Czardom under Ivan Groznyj* (Copenhagen, 1964). Specialized studies that also bear on Ivan are two articles by N. Andreyev: "Kurbsky's Letters to Vas'yan Muromtsev," *Slavonic and East European Review*, XXXIII, no. 81 (June, 1955), 414-436, and "Interpolations in the 16th-Century Muscovite Chronicles," *ibid.*, XXXV, no. 84 (December, 1956), 95-115; one by David Miller: "The Coronation of Ivan IV of Moscow," *Jahrbücher für Geschichte Osteuropas*, XV, no. 4 (December, 1967), 559-574, and another by Oswald P. Backus, "A. M. Kurbsky in the Polish-Lithuanian State (1564-1583)," *Acta Baltico-Slavica*, VI (1969), 29-50. See also J. M. Culpepper, "The Kremlin Executions of 1575 and the Enthronement of Simeon Bekbulatovich," *Slavic Review*, XXIV, no. 3 (September, 1965), 503-506, and the response to his article by Ellerd

Hulbert, "The Zemskii Sobor of 1575: A Mistake in Translation," *ibid.*, XXV, no. 2 (June, 1966), 320-322.

Economic and social developments of the period can be investigated in Jerome Blum, *Lord and Peasant in Russia from the Ninth to the Nineteenth Century* (Princeton, N.J., 1961); and for a broader perspective, see the same author's article, "The Rise of Serfdom in Eastern Europe," *American Historical Review,* LXII (1957), 807-836. An historiographical discussion can be found in George Vernadsky, "Serfdom in Russia," reprinted in S. Harcave, ed., *Readings in Russian History,* vol. I (New York, 1962), 212-228. A Stalinist textbook covering the period has been translated: A. I. Pashkov, ed., *A History of Russian Economic Thought: Ninth through Eighteenth Centuries,* trans. B. Dmytryshyn, R. A. Pierce (Berkeley, 1964). An earlier Soviet treatment is Peter I. Lyashchenko, *History of the National Economy of Russia to the 1917 Revolution,* trans. L. M. Herman (New York, 1949). More recent Soviet scholarship is reviewed by Richard Hellie, "The Foundations of Russian Capitalism," *Slavic Review,* XXVI, no. 1 (March, 1967), 148-154. A recent, concise account of agrarian development up to the sixteenth century is offered by R. E. F. Smith in *The Cambridge Economic History of Europe,* vol. 1 (second edition, Cambridge, 1966), 507-547. A broad, provocative interpretation that expands the conception of a "Time of Troubles" is given by W. H. McNeill, *Europe's Steppe Frontier, 1500-1800* (Chicago, 1964). Some perspective on the problem of famine in Russian history can be gained from Arcadius Kahan, "Natural Calamities and Their Effect upon the Food Supply in Russia (An Introduction to a Catalogue)," *Jahrbücher für Geschichte Osteuropas,* XVI, no. 3 (September, 1968), 353-377. See also the note by G. E. Orchard, "The 'Wasteland' Monasteries: An Historical Revision," *Canadian Slavic Studies,* II, no. 1 (Spring, 1968), 116-119.

Muscovy's relations with the West have formed the focus of several scholarly studies. Walther Kirchner treats Muscovite policy toward the Baltic in his monograph *The Rise of the Baltic Question* (Newark, Del., 1954), and in several articles, recently collected and published as *Commercial Relations between Russia and Europe, 1400 to 1800: Collected Essays* (Bloomington, Ind., 1966). These may be supplemented by Thomas Esper, "Russia and the Baltic, 1494-1558," *Slavic Review,* XXV, no. 3 (September, 1966), 458-474, and the same author's "A Sixteenth-Century Anti-Russian Arms Embargo," *Jahrbücher für Geschichte Osteuropas,* XV, no. 2 (June, 1967), 180-196. Additional studies are by M. Malowist, "Poland, Russia, and Western Trade in the 15th and 16th Centuries," *Past & Present,* no. 13 (April, 1958), 26-41, and by the Soviet historian L. V. Cherepnin, "Russian 17th-Century Baltic Trade in Soviet Historiography," *Slavonic and East European Review,* XLII, no. 100 (December, 1964), 1-22. Polish policy during the Troubles can be followed in F. Nowak, "Sigismund III, 1587-1632," in W. F. Reddaway *et al., The Cambridge History of Poland,* vol. I (Cambridge, 1950). A provocative recent appraisal of Muscovy's military relationship to the West is Thomas Esper's "Military Self-Sufficiency and Weapons Technology in Muscovite Russia," *Slavic Review,* XXVIII, no. 2 (June, 1969), 185-208.

Anglo-Russian relations have attracted continuous scholarly interest. Introduction to the subject and its literature can be gained from M. S. Anderson, *Britain's Discovery of Russia, 1553-1815* (London, 1958); E. J. Simmons, *English Literature and Culture in Russia (1553-1840)* (Cambridge, Mass., 1935); and T. S. Willan, *The Early History of the Muscovy Company, 1553-1603* (Manchester, 1956). A recent publication of letters is Norman Evans's "Queen Elizabeth I and Tsar Boris: Five Letters, 1597-1603," *Oxford Slavonic Papers,* XII (1965), 49-68.

Muscovy and the East are treated in a stimulating symposium on Muscovy and Kazan by Edward Keenan *et al., Slavic Review,* XXVI, no. 4 (December, 1967), 541-583, which covers developments to the mid-sixteenth century. The later decades of the century are explored in W. E. D. Allen, "The Georgian Marriage Projects of Boris Godunov," *Oxford Slavonic Papers,* XII (1965), 69-79; C. M. Kortepeter, "Gazi Giray II, Khan of the Crimea, and Ottoman Policy in Eastern Europe and the Caucasus, 1588-94," *Slavonic and East European Review,* XLIV, no. 102 (January, 1966), 139-166; and A. N. Kurat, "The Turkish Expedition to Astrakhan' in 1569 and the Problem of the Don-Volga Canal," *ibid.,* XL, no. 94 (December, 1961), 7-23. A broad overview is offered in another symposium by Karl A. Wittfogel *et al.,* "Russia and the East," reprinted in D. W. Treadgold, ed., *The Development of the USSR: An Exchange of Views* (Seattle, 1964), 323-358. Two valuable studies of Muscovite expansion into, and rule over, Siberia are: Raymond H. Fisher, *The*

Russian Fur Trade, 1550-1700 (Berkeley, 1943), and G. V. Lantzeff, *Siberia in the Seventeenth Century* (Berkeley, 1943).

Legal and institutional problems have been investigated in a series of articles by Horace W. Dewey: "The 1497 *Sudebnik*—Muscovite Russia's First National Law Code," *American Slavic and East European Review*, XV, no. 3 (October, 1956), 325-338; "Historical Drama in Muscovite Justice: The Case of the Extorted Deed," *Canadian Slavonic Papers*, II (1957), 38-46; "Judges and Evidence in Muscovite Law," *Slavonic and East European Review*, XXXVI, no. 86 (December, 1957), 189-194; "The 1550 *Sudebnik* as an Instrument of Reform," *Jahrbücher für Geschichte Osteuropas*, X, no. 2 (July, 1962), 161-180; "Immunities in Old Russia," *Slavic Review*, XXIII, no. 4 (December, 1964), 643-659; "The Decline of the Muscovite *Namestnik*," *Oxford Slavonic Papers*, XII (1965), 21-39; "Charters of Local Government under Tsar Ivan IV," *Jahrbücher für Geschichte Osteuropas*, XIV, no. 1 (March, 1966), 10-20; "Defamation and False Accusation *(Iabednichestvo)* in Old Muscovite Society," *Slavic and East-European Studies*, XI, nos. 3-4 (1966-67), 109-120; "Old Muscovite Concepts of Injured Honor (Beschestie)," *Slavic Review*, XXVII, no. 4 (December, 1968), 594-603; and with A. M. Kleimola, "Promise and Perfidy in Old Russian Cross-Kissing," *Canadian Slavic Studies*, II, no. 3 (Fall, 1968), 327-341. Also of great value to specialist and nonspecialist alike will be Sergei Pushkarev's *A Dictionary of Russian Historical Terms to 1917*, which was announced for publication in 1969 by the Yale University Press.

Similar issues are examined by Oswald P. Backus, "Theft, Power Structure and Continuity in the History of Russian Law," *Slavic and East-European Studies* (Montreal), VII (1962), 154-184, and "Muscovite Legal Thought, the Law of Theft, and the Problem of Centralization, 1497-1589," in A. D. Ferguson and A. Levin, eds., *Essays in Russian History: A Collection Dedicated to George Vernadsky* (Hamden, Conn., 1964), 35-68. See also J. L. H. Keep, "Bandits and the Law in Muscovy," *Slavonic and East European Review*, XXXV, no. 84 (December, 1956), 201-222, and Henry L. Eaton, "Cadasters and Censuses of Muscovy," *Slavic Review*, XXVI, no. 1 (March, 1967), 54-69.

Cultural and artistic developments can be followed in G. H. Hamilton, *The Art and Architecture of Russia* (London, 1954), and in Arthur Voyce, *Moscow and the Roots of Russian Culture* (Norman, Okla., 1964), and the same author's *The Art and Architecture of Medieval Russia* (Norman, Okla., 1967). On intellectual life (or the lack thereof), see the instructive symposium by Georges Florovsky *et al.*, "Old Russia," reprinted in Treadgold, ed., *The Development of the USSR*, 125-172.

Muscovy in the seventeenth century after the Troubles is studied by J. L. H. Keep, "The Decline of the Zemsky Sobor," *Slavonic and East European Review*, XXXVI, no. 86 (December, 1957), 100-122, and "The Regime of Filaret," *ibid.*, XXXVIII, no. 91 (June, 1960), 334-360. On Russo-Polish relations and the contest for the Ukraine, see L. R. Lewitter, "Poland, the Ukraine, and Russia in the 17th Century," *Slavonic and East European Review*, XXVII, no. 68 (December, 1948), 157-171, no. 69 (May, 1949), 414-429, and the same author's "The Russo-Polish Treaty of 1686 and Its Antecedents," *Polish Review*, IX, no. 4 (Autumn, 1964), 21-36. See also C. Bickford O'Brien, *Muscovy and the Ukraine: From the Pereiaslavl Agreement to the Truce of Andrusovo, 1654-1667* (Berkeley, 1963).

Readers who wish to learn something of contemporary Soviet historiography on topics related to the Time of Troubles, e.g., the recent controversy over the nature of the oprichnina, can consult the journal of reviews entitled *Kritika*, published by advanced graduate students and young faculty at Harvard.

C. Imaginative Literature

Eisenstein's well-known movie "Ivan the Terrible" offers a fascinating study of the period and is now available in book form: S. M. Eisenstein, *Ivan the Terrible, A Screenplay* (New York, 1962). Another famous work is Alexander Pushkin's *Boris Godunov*, trans. P. L. Barbour (New York, 1953); other translations are available, and the play forms the basis of Mussorgsky's classic opera of the same name. An interesting novel about the reign of Ivan the Terrible is A. K. Tolstoi's *Prince Serebryani* (New York, 1892). The same author's play *The Death of Ivan the Terrible* is available in translation by George R. Noyes, ed., *Masterpieces of the Russian Drama* (New York, 1933; reissued in two volumes, New York, 1960). A rather quaint Russian historical novel is by M. N. Zagoskin, *The Young Muscovites; or, The Poles in Russia.* ed. F. Chamier (London, 1833, 3 vols.; New York, 1834, 2 vols.).

Index

Aleksandrova Sloboda, 111

Aliabiev, A. S., 147

Andronov, Feodor, 128

Appanage: definition and structure of, 6-10; annexation by Muscovy, 11-12, 20

Baby Brigand (son of second false Dimitry): origin of, 144; repudiation of him by popular forces, 148, 156-157, 160

Basmanov, Peter Feodorovich: aid to first pretender of, 77-78, 80; murder of, 82

Bekbulatovich, Simeon, 63

Belsky, Bogdan: banishment from Moscow of, 46, 48; claims of, 62-63, 65, 74

Bitiagovsky, Mikhail, 56

"Black lands," 8

Black-soil zone, 33, 37

Bolotnikov, Ivan: revolt of, 93-99; political aims of, 93-94; allies of, 94-95; capture of, 97

Borderland the: Russian colonization of, 34-39; support for Brigand of, 104-105; *See also* Field, the

Boyar Duma, 50, 117, 122, 124, 126, 128, 130, 135

Boyars: definition of, 8; status of, 20-21. *See also* Princely aristocracy

Brigand, the (second false Dimitry): origin of, 102-103; initial invasion by, 105; renewal of campaign of, 105-107; invasion of North by, 108-110; flight from Tushino of, 111-112; threat to Moscow of, 119, 121, 125; murder of, 133; son of, 144

"Brigands": definition of, 93-99. *See*

also Cossacks

Buczynski, Jan, 79

Catholic Church, 70

Charles IX, king of Sweden, 100-101

Cherkassky family, 63, 67

Chodkiewicz, J. C., 152-153

"Chosen Council," 22

Clement VIII, pope, 66

Colonization, 6-8, 27-39

Commune. See *"Mir"*

"Compact" (of June 30, 1611), 138-140

Cossacks: origin and early role of, 34-38; Liapunov's appeals to, 136-138, 140; and destruction of Liapunov, 140-141; and reaction to popular forces, 152-153; role in tsar's election of, 159-162; general role in Troubles of, 168-169

"Deportation": use by Muscovy of, 17-18; role in oprichnina of, 23-24

Desiatinnaia land, 38-39, 71

Deti boyarskie: definition of, 8; mentioned, 18, 25, 37, 114, 116, 120, 128, 136, 155, 167. *See also* Service gentry

Dimitry (first pretender): origin of, 65-70; initial support of, 69-71; and campaign into Muscovy, 74-76; and policy after enthronement, 78-82; murder of, 82

Dimitry (second pretender). *See* Brigand, the

Dimitry, tsarevich: origin and death of, 55-57; dynastic claim of, 57-58; reburial of, 88-89

Dionisy, archimandrite, 144-145

Pozharsky, Dimitry Mikhailovich: and leadership of Nizhny militia, 147; military and political activities of, 149-153; and defeat of Cossacks, 149-150; and role in united provisional government, 153; mentioned, 156, 158

Pretenders, proliferation of, 96. *See also* Brigand, the; Dimitry (first pretender); Dimitry (second pretender); Peter Feodorovich

Prikazy, 136, 139, 168, 174

Princely aristocracy: gradations within, 20-21; and persecution by oprichnina, 20-25; divisions under Feodor of, 47-49; hostility toward Boris of, 54-55; attitude toward Boris of, 64-66; reaction to first pretender of, 68; role in Godunovs' fall of, 77-78; overthrow of first pretender by, 78-84; role in Shuisky's accession of, 86-89; election of Wladyslaw by, 125-126; humiliation by Gosiewski of, 128-130; general role in Troubles of, 164-167. *See also* Boyar Duma; Boyars

Pskov, 14

Razin, Stenka, 169

Riazan: and revolt against Shuisky, 94-95; and mutiny of gentry, 118-119; and revolt against Poles, 134

Romanov, Feodor Nikitich (Filaret): dynastic claims of, 62-64; relations with first pretender of, 66, 68-69; nomination as patriarch of, 83; demotion to metropolitan of, 89; role at Tushino of, 115; arrival in Moscow of, 117-118; opposition to Shuisky of, 121; role in "grand embassy" of, 127; arrest of, 129, 159

Romanov, Ivan Nikitich, 89, 159

Romanov, Mikhail Feodorovich (tsar of Muscovy): election of, 158-162; relations with Zemsky Sobor of, 172-174

Romanov family, 48-49, 54-55, 64, 67-69. *See also* Yuriev, Nikita Romanovich

Romanovna, Anastasia, 54-55, 160

Rozynski, Roman, 102, 104, 106, 111-112

Russian Orthodox Church: opposition to first pretender of, 80-81; opposition to Sigismund of, 131-134

St. George's Day, 9, 29

Saltykov, Ivan Nikitich, 121

Sapieha, Andrzej, 61-62, 65

Sapieha, Jan Peter, 103-107, 144

Sapieha, Leo, 161

Serfdom: Muscovite origins of, 11-12; effects of oprichnina on, 24, 26-27; and competition for labor, 28-30; evolution under Boris of, 53; and legislation under Shuisky, 99-100; Liapunov's measures concerning, 139-140; after the Troubles, 169

Service gentry: definition of, 11; expansion of, 23-26; role in colonization of, 37; position under Boris of, 53; reaction to Bolotnikov of, 94-96; defeat by Cossacks of, 140-141; and election of Mikhail, 158-162; general role in Troubles of, 165-168. *See also Deti boyarskie*

Shakhovskoi, Grigory, 92, 97

Sheremetiev, Feodor Ivanovich, 89, 111

Shuisky, Dimitry Ivanovich, 119, 127

Shuisky, Vasily Ivanovich: report of Uglich tragedy by, 56, 78; opposition to first pretender of, 78-79; and revolt against first pretender, 81-84; accession of, 86-89; relation to mob of, 90-91; and counterattack against Bolotnikov, 95-99; social policies of, 99-100; and re-

buff of Sweden, 100-101; and re-
pulsion of Tushinites, 106-107;
and alliance with Sweden, 108;
and defeat of Tushinites, 110-111;
overthrow of, 118-121; capture of,
127

Shuisky family, 48-49, 61, 64

Sigismund III, king of Poland-
Lithuania: attitude toward Muscovy of, 101-103; and declaration
of war, 112; and attempt at conquest, 127-132; failure of, 154;
rejection of candidacy of, 156-157;
mentioned, 80

Siisky Monastery, 69

Skopin-Shuisky, Mikhail Vasilievich: leadership of counterattack
by, 108; and relief of Moscow,
110-111; victory and death of,
118-119

Soloviev, S. M. (historian): quoted,
8, 119

South, Muscovite. See Borderland,
the; Field, the

Staraia Russa, 14

Streltsy: definition of, 30; mentioned, 37-38, 62, 81, 83, 94, 148,
155, 171

Sweden: proposal to Shuisky of,
100-101; and alliance with Muscovy, 108, 110; reaction to Klushino of, 119; and relations with
popular forces, 151; general role
in Troubles of, 174-176

Sylvester, priest, 22

Tatars, 6, 11, 34-36

Taube, Johann, 26

Teliatevsky, Andrei, 97

Trinity Monastery, 143-146

Trubetskoi, Dimitry: support of
Liapunov by, 134-135, 139-140;
and policy toward popular forces
and Poles, 152-153; mentioned,
145, 156

Trubetskoi, Yury, 93

Tula, 37, 78, 93, 95, 97-99, 104-105

Tushinites: and negotiations with

Sigismund, 112; Russian nobility
among, 113-116; and treaty with
Sigismund, 116-117; and service
under Gosiewski, 128. *See also*
"Brigands"

Tushino, 106-107, 111-117

Uglich, tragedy at, 56-57, 89

Vologda, 31, 110

Vorotynsky, Ivan Mikhailovich, 121

Walled Town, 90, 135, 150, 153

West, the (Europe): Novgorod's relations with, 15-16; and Muscovy,
31-32, 174-176

White Town, 135

Wild Field. *See* Field, the

Wisniowiecki, Adam, 103

Wladyslaw, prince (Sigismund III's
son): candidacy for Muscovy of,
80; election by Tushinites of, 116-
117; his candidacy renewed, 124-
126; Hermogen's reaction to, 132;
his candidacy rejected, 156-157;
continuing claims of, 175

Yaroslavl, 31, 107, 149-152

Yuriev, Nikita Romanovich, 46-47,
54-55, 160

Zamoskovie: definition of, 3; early
history of, 3-6; depopulation of,
27-28, 30-31

Zarutsky, Ivan: support of Brigand
by, 104; support of Liapunov by,
134-135, 139-140; and reaction to
popular forces, 149-150, 152-153;
death of, 169; mentioned, 145

Zemsky Sobor: election of Boris by,
59-60; election of Wladyslaw by,
125-127; election of Mikhail by,
155-162; general role in Troubles
of, 171-174

Zolkiewski, Stanislas: and victory at
Klushino, 119; arrival in Moscow
of, 124-125; policies and retirement of, 127-128; mentioned, 131

Zvenigorodsky, Vasily Andreevich,
147

197